Classic Cars

of Montana & Wyoming

Duane Demars
2007
Enjoy!

Dedication

I dedicate this book to my late parents, who always supported me and my love for cars; my wife, Joanne, who has put up with me and about sixty different cars during our 48 years of marriage; our daughters, Sheri and Brandi; and our granddaughters who were embarrassed to be picked up at school in an old, yellow International pickup with a factory flame job. And yes, they were the first to want a ride in a true "legend," our old 1947 Willys-Overland Jeep in which they later learned how to drive. Finally, we remember with great fondness the thousands of friends we've met through the years who share our love of cars.

— Duane Demars

Foreword

What I have attempted with this book is to showcase as many of the very best classics that Montana and Wyoming have to offer. We owe so very much to icons like Preston Tucker, Henry Ford, Harley Earl and Billings, Montana's own: General Motors chief designer, David North; Lincoln-Mercury senior designer Harvey Markegard; and Chrysler Division senior designer Bruce Ryniker. These men gave us many of the most sought after Classic Cars of today.

To our generation, the automobile has been our path to freedom in ways that our great grandfathers never could have imagined. There is not a man or woman out there today who doesn't remember when they got behind the wheel for the very first time and learned to drive. Only the car enthusiast knows, however, the qualities that go into producing the car of their dreams. There may be a mysterious blend of chrome (or lack of it), coupled with exquisite paint and delicate ghost flames to add to the allure. Often, there are soft and inviting colors or exotic colors that may help to capture the moment. Every classic car owner will put his own touch, his own values and his own personality into his car until it becomes a part of him or her…it is a nurturing process much like a mother's love.

The classic cars of today have taken on a new and very large role in society. We have taken what we have to a whole new level with car shows growing larger, which appeals to families who can have fun and enjoy the cars for free. Almost always, the funds that are raised go to a good cause like a community crisis fund, memorial for a loved one or to help a sick child. Rod runs may be around town or around the state or even the nation. Many clubs have poker runs to raise money. The serious car buff will plan months in advance for the Classic Car shows he or she will attend for the season. With every car show, with every rod and poker run, we recapture our youth. We may like to dress the part, or just sit and visit with old friends. New friends come easily as we all have a common goal, the world of restoring the Classic Cars of days gone by.

Duane Demars

Classic Cars of Montana & Wyoming

by
Duane Demars

website design by
Bill Witcher
www.cars36.com

book design by
Barbara Scheppele
Cooper Creative
www.cooperads.com

Classic Cars of Montana, LLC
Duane Demars
PO Box 50104
Billings, MT 59105

Library of Congress Catalog
Card Number: 2006910311

ISBN - 13: 978-0-9791647-0-5

For additional copies, please contact
Classic Cars of Montana, LLC.

Table of Contents

The vehicles have been added to the book in random order. We could have chosen to place them in order chronologically, by make and model or even alphbetically. Instead we chose to place them randomly so each turn of the page is a surprising glimpse into automotive history.

David North - An Icon of Our Own

David North of Billings, Montana possesses a talent that millions of car lovers wish we had. He can transform a thought into actual design. He discovered this at the early age of 16 while attending Senior High School in the 50s. His talent caught the eye of a General Motors executive who was on vacation and spotted his drawings at a local Cadillac dealership. From that moment, his life changed forever. In 1959, David graduated from the Art Center School of Pasadena, California, long considered the nation's top design school. This launched his stunning career with General Motors that lasted for 33 years and earned him the title of "Chief Designer." It doesn't get any better than that. This man is credited with designing a class of cars that will live on with a lot us who are car lovers. They are the Pontiac GTO and Grand Prix, Oldsmobile Toronado, Cadillac Eldorado, along with the Buick Riviera and the incomparable Buick Reatta. A young man in a vast new world had his career launched to the very top with his design of the GTO, which gained popularity through the years. It is one of the most sought after classics of all time. It began when John Delorean, who was one of the best known engineers in the world, asked David to sketch a back room prototype of what became the muscle car we call the GTO.

The Cord 810, built in 1936, was the first American production car to have front wheel drive. North once said he always had pictures of the Cord around to inspire him. The Toronado has proven to be one of his greatest success stories. Volumes have been written about this car in books all over the world. This car set the trend for the rest of the industry in power, performance and style. It delivers 385 horsepower to the front wheels directly off the assembly line. The Europeans were saying that you could not possibly put more than 200 horsepower to the front wheels without breaking the half shafts. But here was a car that weight 4311 pounds dry. Yet it handled beautifully, even winning the Pikes Peak Hill Climb. The year was 1966 when it became Motor Trend Car of the Year. North credits his styling from a drawing he made in his early 20s known to the automotive world as "The Red Flame." This drawing was made with a stunning scarlet air brush against a jet black background. This car may have been made over 40 years ago; however Jay Leno said he would like to make a modern version of the Toro. He purchased an old beater for $800 and, with his crew and the help of the top General Motors Production Engineers, transformed this stock Toronado into a rear wheel drive with horsepower of 1070 at 6350 rpm using a prototype small block by GM Performance. His feeling is that these cars were designed by guys who went to college. They were professionals who did this for a living. And honestly, as much as I love hot rods, I rarely see a chopped car that looks as nice as stock. You can only imagine the thrill that David North felt in the spring of 2006 when he had the honor to drive this truly great car with Jay Leno sitting in the passenger seat.

In every young man's life will come the time when he has achieved his own rite of passage. This came when the GM executives offered North the chance to design the 1967 Cadillac Eldorado. His father drove a Cadillac and a son's childhood dream of working in the GM division of Cadillac had now come true. North referred to the Cadillac as "The Crown Jewel." He remains a design consultant for General Motors. He also drives a black Cadillac CTS, courtesy of General Motors.

David met the woman he was destined to spend his life with in 1954. Pat and David were both "burning the point" in downtown Billings, Montana, where everyone went to see and be seen. Pat was in a car customized with breather pipes to allow the family dog to ride in the trunk.

A personal note from the author: David and Pat are truly the nicest people one could ever meet. Success has not changed them from who they really are.

Bruce Ryniker

Bruce Ryniker established Durland Productions, Inc., a full-service design, animation, and production company, in 1995 with offices in Torrance and San Diego, California. Durland provides visual concepts and computer animation for a variety of electronic media and has created award-winning games, television commercials, educational and promotional videos. The company is currently producing movie trailers and music videos for several major entertainment industry clients, including Fox, Warner Bros., MGM, Disney, Dreamworks, MTV, and Capitol Records. Recently retired from the positions of President and CEO, Bruce remains active as a board member and design consultant for the company's proprietary product categories consisting of toys, print, and electronic entertainment.

Bruce is an industrial designer with extensive experience in the toy and juvenile products industry, including 20 years with Mattel Toys, Inc., in El Segundo, California as senior design manager for the Boys Toys/Male Action Division. He provided creative direction and team management from inception to production release for both domestic and international product lines within the Male Action, Electronics, and Hot Wheels design groups. He provided on-site manufacturing design support for vendors in Hong Kong, Japan, Mexico, and Canada. He was a member of the team that established facilities and procedures in Tokyo, Japan for the Bandai and Mattel joint research and development venture (B and M Research Group). He coordinated product design, package art, and child-size accessories for the Male Action Division in order to ensure visual continuity during the production of several feature-length films, television series, and electronic games. He also created a variety of original designs for the 1/64-scale die-cast Hot Wheels vehicles, including accessory playsets, racetracks, and special-purpose cars.

Before joining the R&D staff at Mattel, Bruce was involved in the automotive after-market custom and performance industry, creating designs for recreational vehicles, motor homes, movie cars, and automotive accessories, including wheels, engine components, and aerokits. Bruce provided additional concepts for corporate identity programs, package design, and advertising illustration.

From 1966 to 1972, Bruce was an automotive designer on the management staff of Chrysler Corporation in Highland Park, Michigan. He was responsible for a variety of projects from advanced concept studies for prototypes and research vehicles to development design for production automobiles and trucks. He was the designer and project manager for several experimental show cars, including the Chrysler Concept 70x, the Dodge Dart Custom 340, a prototype mid-engine sports car for Plymouth and a high-performance Plymouth Satellite for the NASCAR racing program. His design contributions for production automobiles included the award-winning 1971-1973 Plymouth Road Runner and GTX, and the 1974-1975 Plymouth Fury and Gran Fury. Bruce was also assigned to the International Preproduction Studio developing concepts for Chrysler United Kingdom, France, South Africa, and Australia. Additional projects involved concept and production designs for Dodge Truck Division, ranging from pickups and SUVs to aerodynamic studies for transport vehicles and mass transit systems. And then for something completely different, he designed vehicles without any wheels at all, creating watercraft and speedboats for Chrysler Marine Division.

From 1963 to 1966, Bruce was an automotive designer for General Motors Corporation in Warren, Michigan, involved in various stages of vehicle evolution from concept exploration to production feasibility. He provided design solutions for Chevrolet and GMC truck lines, including show trucks, station wagons, and sports utility vehicles, a V-16 powered show car for Cadillac, an experimental four-wheel drive mid-engine Corvette, and advanced vehicle concepts for the 1964 World's Fair Futurama exhibit. He participated in General Motors Institute Specialized Technical Education Program for automotive engineering from 1963 to 1966.

Bruce graduated from the Art Center College of Design in Pasadena, California, where he was awarded a Ford scholarship and received a Bachclor of Professional Arts degree in transportation design.

Bruce is a subject of biographical reference in the Marquis Who's Who in the World, Who's Who in Science and Industry, and the American Biographical Institutes Personalities of the West and Midwest.

Bruce Ryniker and his wife, Marilee, are native Montanans now living in Billings.

1955 Chevrolet Bel Air Sport Coupe
Ed & Linda Randash, Owners

350 Cubic inch LT-1, Ford 9" differential, 17" and 18" wheels

The 1955 Chevrolet, called "The Hot One," are most desired as collectibles due to their styling. Harley Earl's hallmark was present in the wrap-around windshield. The inspiration for the egg-crate grill came from Ferrari and was known as one of Earl's favorite touches. Adding to the popularity of the 1955 was a more capable steering system, bigger brakes and better suspension. These cars had better visibility and more interior room with a very large trunk, In 1955, Chevy was able to lead the industry with a record year by producing more than 1.7 million cars. This was a new high for the marquee and 250,000 units greater than Ford.

— Ed & Linda Randash
Billings, Montana

1957 Chevrolet Bel Air
Ed & Linda Randash, Owners

Two Door Post, Engine ZZ-4, Transmission R-700, Ford 9" rear end, Morrison Frame, 18" & 20" wheels and tires, leather interior with a decked hood.

The 1957 Chevrolet came with seven engine choices, of which five were 283s ranging in horsepower from 185 to 283 brake horsepower. These cars could go from 0-60 in 9.9 seconds, the quarter-mile was reached in 17.5 seconds and reaching 110 mph flat out. This car became a formidable track competitor as Chevy came to be regarded in many circles as the definitive car of the 1950s. Even today, this car enjoys the spotlight as one of the cars most loved by everyone.

— Ed & Linda Randash
Billings, Montana

1963 Corvair Monza
Wanda Nelson, Owner

The Corvair, made by Chevrolet, was first produced in 1960 for the American public who wanted economy in a compact car. In 1963, there were only 36,693 of these produced. Starting in 1956, the Corvair was the dream of the chief engineer Edward N. Cole. This new 900 convertible was a real attention getter, it boasted an upscale interior featuring bucket seats and had the looks and feel of a sport car. The car buyer was looking for economy and found it in the Corvair.

— Owner: Wanda Nelson
Restoration: S & L Classics
Mills, Wyoming

Big Names in Automotive History

David Buick - A plumbing inventor and manufacturer built his first car in 1900.

Antoine Cadillac - Founded the City of Detroit in the 17th century.

Louis Chevrolet - A Swiss race car driver and engineer built his first car in 1911 with financing by William Durant.

Walter Chrysler - A locomotive mechanic who got into the automobile business in 1912 and publicly displayed his own first car at the 1924 NY Auto Show and selling an amazing 32,000 cars in his first year.

E.L. Cord - As General Manager of Auburn Auto Company, he produced some of the most advanced (front-wheel drive, supercharged V8's) and beautiful cars ever under his own name. Unfortunately, they were expensive and came along during the start of the Depression.

Gottlieb Daimler - Can be considered as the founder of the automobile industry when he formed Daimler Motor Company in 1890.

John & Horace Dodge - Their first car came off the assembly line in 1914. Both brothers died within less than a year of each other during the influenza epidemic in 1920.

Harley Earl - Designed the La Salle in 1927, the beginning of a trend toward lower and wider cars. As head of GM's styling department he invented the tail fin and designed the Corvette.

Enzo Ferrari - A mechanic, race car driver then race car team owner. His cars dominated racing for many years after WWII.

Harvey Firestone - His tires went on the first mass-produced Fords.

Henry Ford - In creating the assembly line for automobiles he also created jobs for thousands and affordable cars for millions. What Henry did for automobiles spilled over into other consumer goods.

BF Goodrich - The company started in 1896 has many firsts: First synthetic rubber tire, first tubeless tire, first American-made radial tire, the first space-saver spare and the first "run flat" tire.

Charles Goodyear - Accidentally discovered the rubber vulcanizing process. He patented the process, but couldn't come up with any practical uses for it and died penniless in 1860. The Goodyear Tire and Rubber Company was named after him.

Soichiro Honda - With just $3,300 to his name, he started making motorcycles after WWII.

Emile Jellinek - In 1900, while a Daimler Motor Works board member, Jellinek convinced Gottlieb Daimler to build a race car and name it after Emile's daughter, Mercedes.

Ransom Olds - His highly successful "Curved Dash" runabout put Michigan on the map as a source of motor vehicles. He soon left his namesake company. Later he produced the first gasoline lawn mower.

Ferdinand Porsche - A design engineer who never created a car carrying his name. That was left to his son, Ferry, to accomplish.

Frederick Royce & Charles Rolls - Engineer Royce and car dealer Rolls introduced their first car in 1904.

Preston Tucker - After WWII Tucker designed, built and promoted an innovative car with features, power, and aerodynamic design never before seen and at a very good price. His company folded after building 51 cars.

1947 Ford Business Coupe

Rick & Sue Carnahan, Owners

This totally custom 1947 Ford Business Coupe has been restored from the frame up. It features a Fat Man custom independent front suspension system and a Ford nine-inch rear end. This beauty has a small block 350/375 hp crate motor, automatic transmission, power disc brake, and power steering. It even has a full Vintage Air system. As if that weren't enough, we went as far as to add power windows, 9-way power seats, a custom interior, and CD/DVD player with premium sound package. There are 16" front, and 17" rear American Racing Torg Thrust II wheels. The front and rear bumpers have been smoothed and the coupe has been lowered to 3" off of the ground. Meticulous attention has been paid to every detail of this restoration. While we went to great lengths to get the best picture of this car, photos don't do it justice. This 1947 Coupe looks as if it never left its garage. Its pristine appearance is maintained with regular detailing. We believe the interior and exterior of this old coupe are unblemished and in mint condition.

— Rick & Sue Carnahan
Great Falls, Montana

1955 Mercury Montclair SunValley

Jack & Beverly Willson, owners

Truly a gem to behold !! This beautiful 1955 Mercury SunValley 2-door hardtop with a glass roof is one of the most cherished of all classics. Jack and Bev Willson are the 3rd owners of this car. It spent the first 30 years of its life in the Yankton, South Dakota area. For the next 20 years, the Willson's slowly accumulated parts and completed a frame-off restoration on their Glen Lake metallic blue prize. This car has 43 of the 45 factory options of power equipment offered by Mercury in 1955. The car was finished in June of 2005, at which time it was taken to Denver, Colorado for the AACA Grand National Awards Meet. It won a Junior First award, which is the highest award attainable for its first show. In September of 2005, this car was entered in the Miles City, Montana show with over 100 cars in competition. It was awarded all 3 top trophies including Best Original car from 1955 to 1961. Best Original Restored FOMOCO car at the show along with the People's Choice First Place Trophy.

There were only 1787 of these cars made in 1955, they weighed 3560 pounds and sold for a base price of $2712 without all the options offered.

— Jack & Bev Willson
Ekalaka, Montana

1956 Thunderbird
Dick & DJ Rosekelly, Owners

Dick and DJ Rosekelly purchased this beautiful 1956 T-Bird in 1980. It has been kept in its original factory condition. This red Thunder Bird has two tops — a hard top and a soft top. Mr. Jim Schmid, who is a professional mechanic, rebuilt the power train to factory specifications. Mr. Don Lennick was chosen to refurbish the interior and redo the soft top for the car. The battery, tires and carpet all meet factory specs.

This V8, with an automatic transmission, produces 225 brake horsepower. The car sold new for $3,151.00 and weighed 3,038 pounds. Only 15,631 of these cards were produced in 1956.

1975 Cadillac Eldorado
Dick & DJ Rosekelly, Owners

This 1975 Cadillac Eldorado convertible can almost be classified as a survivor except for the replacement of a new factory soft top. The original top was damaged when the car was loaded with antiques from a road trip. The weather was very hot and when they decided to put the top down, the rear glass shattered, as there was no room to lower it — a hard lesson learned. This car was purchased in 1978 and driven very little up to now. When gas was about $.35 per gallon, the 13-MPG was not all that bad. It has a 500 CID engine and response time from a dead start was like a semi truck. The big engine only produced 190 brake horsepower with a top speed of 109 mph. It came with a 126-inch wheelbase and a weight of 5,167 pounds. There were only 8,950 produced and each carried a price tag of $10,354.00.

— Dick & DJ Rosekelly

1972 Chevrolet Malibu

Ed & Becky Gergen, Owners

We purchased this car in 2004 from the original owner, who purchased it in 1972 off the showroom floor of Lohman Motors in Miles City, Montana. We found the build sheet in the car, which verified all numbers.

The car is "all original" from the vinyl roof down to the original tires. The mileage on this car is less than 6,100 miles. It is equipped with a 350 CID 4-barrel, automatic transmission, power steering with factory air and a tilt steering wheel. The inside upholstery is in new condition along with the carpet. The original AM eight-track still works.

We have been showing this car for the past year in the "Survivor" class along with the "Original GM" class at various car shows.

– Ed & Becky Gergen
Miles City, Montana

1958 Chevrolet Cameo Pickup
Janet Bergman, Owner

My 1958 Chevrolet Cameo pickup was found in Miami, Oklahoma. It was in drivable condition, but I chose to have it trucked to Billings, Montana. The original classy color combo was turquoise and black, which were the colors I wanted.

In researching this vehicle, I found that there were only 1,405 models made and they sold for $2,231.00

Mark Tronstad put my '58 Chevy Cameo back to its original condition. I cannot thank him enough for all of his hard work and patience.

—Janet Bergman
Billings, Montana

1967 CHEVROLET NOVA

SHANNON PURVIANCE, OWNER

The love that I have for cars is expressed through this 1967 Chevy Nova, which I started as a project car about 1996. The dream of building the car that I have always wanted has now become a reality. We seem to put ourselves, or better yet our own personality, into what we love the most. Eddie Franklin completed the body and the perfect paint job. The flames were the work of a true master, being designed by Wade Shanafelt. The interior of the car, which has a very unique head liner, was completed by Freak Nasty of Casper, Wyoming.

The engine is a 327 cubic inch coupled with a turbo 350 transmission and a 3:73 posi-track rear end. The 300-watt stereo will let you know we are coming.

This car new sold for about $2590 and carried a weight of 2820 pounds.

— Shannon Purviance
Douglas, Wyoming

1932 Hupmobile - model 216-B
Scott Remus - Owner

There are only 9 of these beauties registered. I found this car in Fort Collins, Colorado in a garage where it sat for 35 years. I began my restoration by powder coating the frame. All of the original suspension was used. The body, which is wood frame, was found to be in very good condition. I treated the wood to retain its original construction. The body remains completely uncut and unchanged. The car has drum brakes, no heater or air conditioner and no windshield wipers. I reworked the wiring and steering column, added new gauges, race seats and more interior wood. There was no rust found on the body. The motor is a small block Chevy with a 700R4 transmission. The body work and painting took about two months. I AM ONE LUCKY GUY!

— Scott Remus
Loveland, Colorado

1939 Ford Standard 5-Window Coupe

Stan Bradley, Owner

Cars of this time were the most memorable of the era. The styling of this car evolved around designer Bob Gregorie under the ever present eye of Edsel Ford, who at that time was President of the Ford Motor Company. When this car was made, it had the Henry Ford unassuming cast iron flathead V8. The 222 cubic inch 90 horsepower made this one of the hottest cars on the road and was termed as one of the best engines of its day. The price tag, when new, was an astounding $640.00 and the car weighed 2,710 pounds.

We tend to add our personal touch to what we enjoy, as with this 39 Ford. It has a 400 HP 327 Chevrolet engine, stick shift with a stall converter. A 12-bolt 1974 Camaro rear end has also been added. This car originated in Hamburg, Pennsylvania

— Stan Bradley
Grass Range, Montana

1937 Plymouth Viper Red
Gary & Patti Ugrin, Owners

The 1937 Plymouth has a great history. It was a success from its debut in 1928 and prospered because of a low price, attractive styling and engineering that was more advanced than Ford or Chevrolet. Plymouth never out produced Ford or Chevrolet, but was able to firmly establish itself as the number three car in America, a spot it held until the 1950s. It was an all steel body in a time when wood frame bodies were the norm. New items were added like hydraulic brakes, standard safety glass, and a concealed heater complete with new recessed controls. In 1937 there were 552,000 cars produced — complete with suicide doors — which was also the first time the price tag rose above $1,000.00.

This Viper Red car was purchased out of Ohio in very good condition. It has a 383 Magnum engine, 727 Torque Flight automatic transmission, with a 2.76 rear end. This car has VDO gauges, power steering, tilt wheel, and, not to be forgotten, the classic crank out windshield. The interior has been done in a charcoal velour cloth, which is also classic to this era of car.

— Gary & Patti Ugrin
Billings, Montana

1961 Chevrolet 2 Door Hard Top

Tim & Mindy Brocopp, Owners

The lines of the 1961 Chevy Impala were smooth and not as pronounced as earlier models. Taut new finless styling had arrived. Chevrolet followed the marketing strategy of Ford for several years during the 60s and yet continued to out pace their production each year. They did this with a winning team of designers who came out on top every model year except 1966. The era's most beautiful big Chevy might just be the 1961 hard top with its sculptured lines like a raised convertible top. Starting with 1966, all the automakers were trying to make a car that would appeal to every market they could think of.

This car was purchased new in August of 1961. Tim and Mindy became the second owners in 1998. Even though the car was in very good condition, it under went a frame-off restoration. This original looking hard top has a 348 cubic-inch engine and a 4-speed transmission. The rear end is still the original that was in the car. Body work and painting was done by Kevin Van Larrshoven. Don's upholstery did a top quality job which adds to the beauty of this Chevy.

— Tim & Mindy Brocopp
Billings, Montana

1932 Ford Sedan Delivery
Don & Marilyn Brocopp, Owners

This 32 Ford is truly a gem that can compete with the very best at any car show in the nation. I would simply describe it as perfection at every level and is one of only 26 known to exist in the United States. This reader board tells all about the work that went into this frame-off restoration.

— Don & Marilyn Brocopp
Billings, Montana

1950 Ford F-1 Pickup

Jeff Richardson, Owner

Trucks of the postwar years were some of the best ever made. This truck, belonging to Jeff Richardson, is no exception. Rugged style and durability is the hallmark of this classic. He restored this F-1 in 1982 only to update it in 2000 – to a certain point. It has a 302 V8 with a B&M Blower, a C-6 automatic transmission with a Ford 9 inch 3:55 gears. The front suspension is a Mustang ll IFS, giving it a lowered look and great handling ability. He used the original stock seat with crushed velvet covering. This pickup is known to all the car buffs as the Green Lizard. Ford spent $1,000,000 to design and tool this cab with the comfort of your best arm chair. Ford styling rebounded from the 1947 models with a popular multi-horizontal grill.

—Jeff Richardson
Billings, Montana

1967 Pontiac Firebird Convertible
Mike & Frieda Tyler, Owners

When Mike & Frieda located this 1967 Pontiac Firebird Convertible in 1992, it was in running condition. However, a lot of long hours were needed to restore it to its pristine condition. The winter that followed proved to be just what the owner of this classic car needed to complete its transformation into a show car. This Firebird 400 convertible came with tri powered carburation, automatic transmission and a 3.23 posi-traction rear end. It was equipped with factory air conditioning, power top, windows, antenna, and a factory tach mounted on the hood, all new to this era. When this car was made in June of 1967, it had power steering, tilt wheel, spoiler and a console clock as part of the 400 package. Off the assembly line, it would do 0 to 60 mph in just 6.2 seconds with a top speed in the quarter mile of 98 mph in just under 14.4 seconds. This car cost about $3800 equipped, with only 15,528 made in this production year.

— Mike & Frieda Tyler
Moore, Montana

1974 Chevrolet Nova

David Canfield, Owner

This 1974 Chevrolet Nova has been more or less changed into a 1970 Nova Super Sport. I purchased this car from the original owners in California in 1966. It was the original beige color, rust free, without any dents or dings, with 69,000 actual miles. I have been working on this car for the last ten years in my spare time. It has a new 383 cubic inch stroker motor that is balanced and blueprinted. I added a steel crank, 202 heads with 3 angle stainless steel valves, roller rockers and gear drive. I used a radical cam and a close ratio 4 speed manual transmission. The front suspension is new with disk brakes. The interior is new with a custom dash, gauges and air conditioning.

About 13,200 were produced selling new for about $2,435.00. Based on the weight it would cost about $1.15 per pound.

— David Canfield
Trout Creek, Montana

1964 Ford Falcon Sprint

Bret Ortgies, Owner

In 1964, the Ford Falcon Sprint came into its own when it appeared in the Monte Carlo Rally and finished second overall. Another Ford Falcon won in the GT class. In 1964, with a 109.5-inch wheelbase, the Falcon got its first major re-styling. This sporty two-door hardtop has a 302 cubic-inch, V8 racing engine.

Bret first spotted this car at a show in August, 2000. It had so caught his eye, he felt like it was the only car at the show. Indeed, there was a lot of work to be done, however, he knew it had a lot of potential and knew it was the only car he wanted. The engine had to be rebuilt. Body rust was repaired along with most everything else. The factory 4-speed and 3:08 rear end were in good shape. Kevin's Customs of Billings painted it "Night Train Red." Mangum's of Laurel, Montana completed the upholstery.

—Bret Ortgies
Billings, MT

1967 Pontiac GTO

Augie & Patsy Bentz, Owners

The age of the muscle cars can best be described by the 1967 GTO. Some were faster, however none had the GTO's panache. It came with a 389 cubic inch 360 horse power that could accelerate from 0 to 60 MPH in just 6.6 seconds. It could run the quarter mile in just 14.4 seconds at speeds up to 99 MPH. Pontiac produced 782,734 cars in 1967 with only 65,176 destined to become GTOs. Sports car enthusiasts took exception to the term GTO (gran turismo omologato) an Italian term referring to production racing cars. One publication came to Pontiac's defense and compared the GTO to the Ferrari. (Quote) "It will beat it on a drag strip and will lose on the race track." The Ferrari, in 1967, cost $20,000 compared to Pontiac at $2,935. The '67 had a three inch longer body, smoother contour lines with coke bottle rear fenders. Finding a GTO today can become very difficult as they are one of the most sought after of the classic cars.

— Augie & Patsy Bentz
Billings, Montana

1968 Ford Torino GT
Chris Palmer, Owner

I purchased my 1968 Ford Torino GT during April, 2002 and drove everywhere during that long, hot summer, with only minor repairs having to be done. When the spring of 2003 came, I decided some serious work had to be done if I was going to make this Torino into the car of my dreams. I started with a new cam and intake manifold. Within the next two months I completed a rebuild on this 390 cubic inch engine and transmission. After I had the front suspension completely gone through, I waited until 2004 to have my car repainted its original color with Seafoam Green paint. By 2005, I completed my new interior, carpets and had a lot of my chrome refinished. This car has all Ford accessories and options, which all work as they should. It turned out better than I could ever imagined, and I love driving it as much as I can. The Torino GT had it all, more performance options than any dealer could possibly remember. There were only 35,964 of these cars made selling for $2,710.00 new and weighing in at 3,098 pounds.

— Chris Palmer
Glendive, Montana

1957 Chevrolet Pickup
Mike & Katie Mills, Owners

We became the second owners of this Indian Turquoise 1957 Chevrolet Pickup when we purchased it from the original owner in October, 1991. This pickup was bought to repair and haul lawn mowers for a high school business, something that it has never done. June of 1994 brought the completion of a ground-up restoration after countless hours and many mowed lawns!

Mike's '57 has been a continual project ever since we declared it finished. In 1998, we added a 350 turbo transmission and custom console. In the summer of 2000, we added a Camaro sub-frame, tilt steering and a 10-bolt posi-traction rear end. Unable to leave well enough alone, we removed the 283 in 2004 and replaced it with a tunnel ram 355 small block. This pickup is enjoyed and driven often by both Katie and me. A big *thank you* to my parents and Clint's Restoration.

Mike & Katie Mills
Glendive, Montana

1967 Corvette Sting Ray
Scott & Ann Mills, Owners

Our Daytona Yellow 1967 Corvette coupe has been a much-enjoyed member of our family for nearly 30 years. It was Goodwood Green when it left the GM factory, but repainted yellow only a few years later. The saddle-tan interior and yellow paint were redone in the early 90s when the car was restored. Hallibrad polished 5-spoke wheels were added in 2005.

The original 390 horsepower 427 engine (on an engine stand) shares garage space with the car, but for now our Corvette runs more economically and is more street worthy with a 350 horsepower 327. It has a 4-speed transmission and factory side pipes. By 1967, the Sting Ray was virtually perfected, the only changes were a single, oblong light above the license plate, bolt-on rather than knock-off aluminum wheels and revised front fender louvers. This car sold new for about $4,343, with a production of only 8,504 that year.

Original air conditioning makes cruising very comfortable and summertime finds us driving our Corvette to many events both near and far.

— Scott & Ann Mills
Glendive, Montana

1967 Ford Mustang Convertible
David C. Anderson, Owner

The best way to describe this 1967 Mustang Convertible when it was found would be "Basket Case." In truth, it was only a shell. What a difference a complete frame-off restoration made. Bodywork and paint was completed by a master at both, Jim Garretson, who placed ghost Mustangs on the hood, doors and the trunk. The Ford 351 Windsor engine was blue printed and balanced using Chevrolet oversized valves, rockers with an Edelbrock carburetor and intake manifold. The transmission is an automatic coupled with a stock rear end. A deeper grille, revised tail lamps, and sculptured side panels that come together with twin simulated air scoops, mark the 1967 Mustang. When this car was made, there were 44,808 produced and sold for $2,698.00 and weighing only 2,738 pounds.

— David C. Anderson
Billings, Montana

1969 Chevelle Malibu
Paul & Debra Nardella, Owners

We purchased this car from its original owner in 1978. The original owner drove this beauty off the show room floor at City Chevrolet in Great Falls, Montana. We started our total frame-off restoration in 1995, which became a lengthy process. We finished it in 2005. During this time, we installed a new, crated 454 cubic-inch engine and had a new custom interior designed. We have kept the original color for this stunning convertible.

Production of Chevelle Malibu's convertible with a V8 in 1969 totaled just 27,300 and sold for $2,743.00. Freight would add about $275.00 to the cost delivered to Montana.

— Paul & Debra Nardella
Livingston, Montana

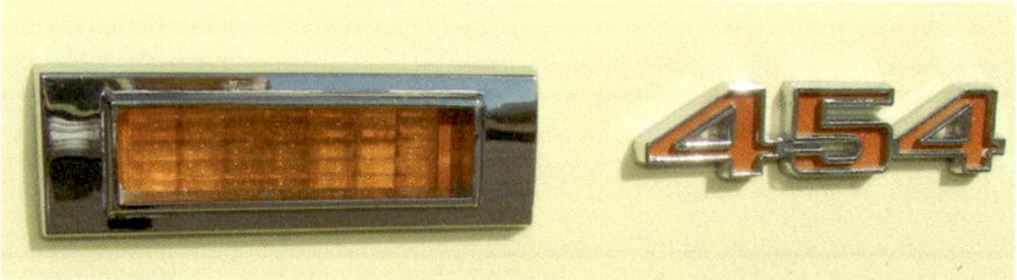

1957 Chevrolet Bel Air

Don & Marilyn Brocopp, Owners

The car-buying public gave this 1957 Chevrolet their greatest compliment with the words "sweet, smooth, and sassy." When this car came off the production line with Ed Cole's Turbo-Fire V8, it became the first production engine to make one horsepower per cubic inch. The Bel Air became the king of the street with production that broke the barrier of 1.5 million cars and made Ford run to try to catch up. These are among the most coveted cars by collectors because they reflect the mid-fifties for all of us. General Motors produced 166,426 Bel Air 2-door hard tops, which they sold for just $2,299.00. At 3,360 pounds, this car cost $1.46 per pound. This restoration was completed in 1998 and has been driven around 3,500 miles per year to classic car shows throughout the west.

— Don & Marilyn Brocopp
Billings, MT

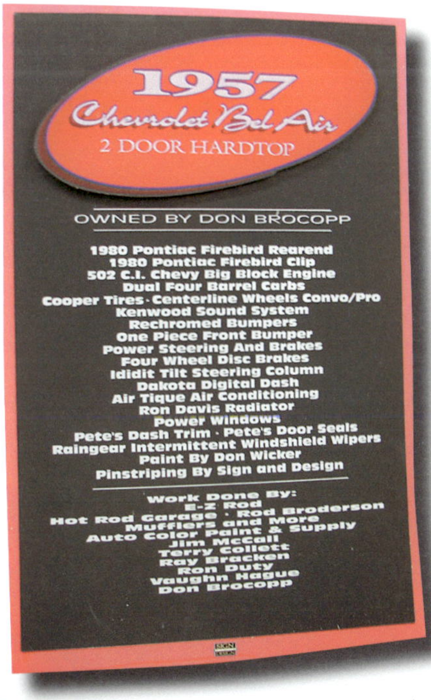

1983 DeLorean
Jeff Richardson, Owner

The Delorean was a unique brushed stainless steel sports car. It was the dream of one of General Motors' most respected designers. After working his way to the top of the design field, John DeLorean decided to reach for the sky. He decided to go it alone and build a lightweight sports car to show the top builders of the world that he had what it takes. He left General Motors in 1973 to pursue the Delorean sports car, which was intended to give the motoring world a taste of the future. This car did just that when it was featured in the movie "Back To The Future," starring Michael J. Fox. The gull wing had the styling to compete with the best. John DeLorean was a tall man with a good tan and the influence of a great salesman. He convinced the British government to give him $130,000,000. The cars were built from 1981 to 1983 in West Belfast, before his financial world came apart and he was $50,000,000 in debt. The overhead-cam, Volvo-sourced 2.8 V6 rear engine used a Bosch K-Jetronic fuel injection. It had a five speed transmission with an optional three speed automatic.

Jeff is only the second owner of this piece of automotive history. He traded a Ford Bronco for this car and then re-purchased the Bronco — some things we just cannot part with.

— Jeff Richardson
Billings, Montana

1972 CHEVROLET CHEYENNE

ALAN & SHARON BULL, OWNERS

On our way back from Las Vegas, as we drove through Sheridan, Wyoming, we spotted this beautiful 1972 Chevrolet Cheyenne pickup. We fell in love and purchased it on the spot, largely because it was in such great shape. The power train has a 402 big block, coupled with a 400 automatic transmission and a 323 rear end. We hired Triple T Inc. to paint our classic a stunning black. Although it may be in top shape, we intend to do a frame-off restoration or at least a major up grade in the near future. When I arrived home with our new purchase, I asked my wife to pull it into the garage. A very loose cam had allowed it to idle at 13 -15 hundred RPM. By the time she got it running and in gear she was headed for the garage where she got half way in before it stalled. The long and narrow of it is, I had two black marks on the floor where the truck went sideways and almost hit the garage door opening. She doesn't drive it much any more.

— Alan & Sharon Bull
Billings, Montana

2005 Ford F-350 Harley Davidson Edition

Frank Miller, Owner

Named "Mans Ruin," this is a class act. This 2005 Ford F-350 Harley Davidson Edition #2416 was being built for the world class SEMA Automotive Show.

The equipment is as follows: Kellerman 12" Air Ride Lift, Super Star wheels by KD with 43" Nitro tires. Pioneer Sound System with GPS, DVD with 6 monitors in dash, head rest and external cased. Sound system done by Rob at Hayloft Auto, fabrication by Steve of Fabcraft, lights by PIAA, running boards and rear step by ATS, push bar by Westin, Banks 4" exhaust system, design by Hayloft Graphics & Design, air brushed by Matt Hubbard, power coating by Armor Power Coating, parts & assembly by Hayloft Autobody & Sales.

If you want a high-rise view of a race, the aluminum box rises 9 feet in the air, complete with video and sound recording equipment. Open the door and a step drops down for easy entry. Many of the items featured are specially made for this truck. The murals painted on each side are true works of art featuring the Viet Nam War on one side and the Hayloft Girls along with racing cars on the other.

— Frank Miller
Lolo, Montana

1950 Chevrolet Deluxe 2-Door Post

Duane & Joanne Demars, Owners

We purchased this 1950 Chevrolet Deluxe 2-door in 2000, when we found it in a grove of timber. It had been there for 25 years with no brakes. We installed a battery, put some gas in the carburetor and it started up. "Bustle Back" was the name General Motors gave this 2-door sedan. GM produced 248,567 of these beauties and sold them for $1,482.00 each. Restoration included a 305 high-performance Chevy small block, A/C, turbo 350 automatic, new paint, interior and glass. My wife came up with the slogan "Relivin' the 50's" for the trunk of the car. This car was popularized as the "workingman's car" during the 1950s. The cost difference between the deluxe and standard — $18.00.

—Duane & Joanne Demars
Billings, MT

1935 Pontiac Business Coupe
Augie & Patsy Bentz, Owners

This 1935 Pontiac is a work of art from the famous Indian Chief head molded into the door panels of the suicide doors to the stunning silver paint that glistens in the sunlight. A complete frame-off restoration has made this an award winning show car. Pontiac, founded in 1926, proved to be one of the most successful of General Motors' divisions. It was a step up from the Chevrolet, which placed it in the same class as Buick and Oldsmobile and became a top seller in the United States. Production reached over 200,000, which in terms of General Motors, was considered an instant success. New independent suspension and Silver Streak styling added even more to its allure for the car buyer.

— Augie & Patsy Bentz
Billings, Montana

1971 Pontiac LeMans

Tom Wood & Linda Niemi, Owners

Linda and I purchased this 1971 Pontiac LeMans December 31, 2005, in Great Falls, Montana, and the work began. Here is a list of what we did to make this our dream car:

Shaved door handles
Autometer gauges
Ididit steering column
Air conditioning
389 gears
Pertronix distributor
Tubbed rear fender wells
Coil over rear shocks with 150 pound rating
Interior: Miller's Upholstery, Great Falls, MT
Custom made dash
Aluminum radiator
Flexlite cooling fans
Full roll cage
Turbo 400 transmission
4-wheel disk brakes
Fuel cell
Painless wiring system
B&M shifter
March pulley system
Narrowed Ford 9" rear axle
Crane 8mm wire set
16" wide rear tires
Procar seats
Electric exhaust cutouts on 3" exhaust
Original Parts door panels

We had the car painted in Pennsylvania. Ninety-nine percent of the work was done in our shop north of Joplin, Montana. Future endeavors: Tunes and a 700 R 4 transmission.

— Tom Wood & Linda Niemi
Joplin, Montana

1955 Chevrolet Bel Air
Ray & Roxanne Bracken, Owners

With the production of the 1955 Chevrolet, the phrase "Double Nickel" started. It referred to the 55, 56, 57 Chevy's. These three years of production have been the most popular years ever for Chevrolet Classics. General Motors spent over $40,000,000 to retool for what was to be one of their greatest design changes. It would be recognized by the automotive world as the definitive car of the 50s. The properly equipped 1955 was a major fast track competitor, only to have Chevys withdrawn from racing in 1957. When Ray & Roxanne purchased this, calling it a "fixer-upper" would have been polite. Most would have just thrown up their hands and looked for a better car. Ray, however, saw a diamond in the rough that few people could see. He started with a frame-off restoration in 1997. It took about five years, many long nights and lost weekends to create the classic car he always wanted. It now has a 350 cubic-inch engine with a 350 turbo transmission and a Pontiac rear end. The Pontiac sub frame provides a modern suspension. He added air conditioning and Don's Custom Upholstery did the interior. Ron Hennley did the body work and crafted a paint job much better than factory.

— Ray & Roxanne Bracken
Billings, Montana

1936 Ford Sedan
Rollie & Dee Dee Topp, Owners

This 1936 Ford four-door sedan was truly a work of art, designed for the workingman. We purchased this completed sedan in June of 2006. We wanted a classic we could enjoy now, not later in life. This car had a full frame-off restoration and at that time the decision was made to do a major upgrade. A 350 cubic-inch Chevrolet small block was installed along with a 350 turbo automatic transmission and an 8-inch rear end. The Mustang suspension allowed for power steering and disk brakes, allowing that smooth ride we all love.

We now are able to attend the classic car shows that we have only read about in the papers or heard about from our friends. It's a way we choose to relive our youth and just reflect back on life with the cars of the past.

— Rollie & Dee Dee Topp
Baker, Montana

1967 Ford Mustang Hard Top
David C. Anderson, Owner

A 1967 Mustang in a field with out any hood, fenders or an engine — and mice rearranging what was left of the interior — is still a Mustang. It was longing to become a show car in the world of classic cars; a car to be admired by all. The body was just rusting away and would have become just another old relic had I not spotted it. I did as much of the bodywork as I could, starting with a frame-off restoration. Thanks to Larry Lees' professional help, we were able to complete the rest of the job. We installed a 351 Windsor engine, an Edelbrock carburetor and intake manifold. This car came with factory air conditioning — not that many were made with this option in '67. It was completed by Jim Garretson of A-AA Auto Body, who used Ford Electric Red paint to make the statement "I'm back!" He punctuated that statement with breath-taking ghost Mustangs on the side, hood and trunk. Ford production of this hard top coupe reached 356,271 this year and sold for $2,461.00

— David C. Anderson
Billings, Montana

1973 Ford Mustang
Jeff Richardson, Owner

This 1973 Mustang underwent several major changes starting in the 1970s. It became larger, heavier, and thirstier. This Mustang would be as fat as it would ever get. The wheelbase was extended 1 inch, the width was widened 6 inches and it gained 600 pounds over the original 1964 weight. The styling became more massive, the sheet metal was busier, even the nose was more aggressive with a sweeping design. With the increase in size, came room for even larger engines like the 351 Cleveland in this car, which is equipped with an automatic and shift kit.

Adding to the driving pleasure is the 9-inch limited slip rear end. The interior remains in excellent condition with the comfort weave and vinyl it came with. It was painted in 1983 with black delstar, gold pearl and gold mica. The vinyl, padded roof has a single stitch French seam with recessed Grande emblem. Adding to the beauty is the Keystone Classic wheels with BF Goodrich tires. Only 25,274 were produced and sold for $2,946.00. This Grande Hard Top Coupe weighed 3,059 pounds.

—Jeff Richardson
Billings, Montana

1950 Studebaker Starlight Coupe

Ronn & Linda Duty, Owners

The 1950 Studebaker had an appealing new design, which can be credited to the Lowery - Exner Studios design team. Styling was to be the best selling point despite all the jokes like "which way is it going?" This innovative design eliminated the bolt-on fenders that were on the pre-war cars. This envelope body made it possible to extend the front seat width six inches and the back seat ten inches, giving excellent room inside. Studebaker's shape and design made it one of the most advanced cars on the highway. The year 1950 proved to be the very best year for production of the Studebaker line. These cars were first offered to the public after WW II. Automobile production ground to a halt during the war because of the need for steel. Unlike today's cars, which are built mostly of plastic, cars were made of good, old American steel. This Champion body sat on a 113-inch frame, weighed 2,705 pounds and cost $1,582.00 new.

Ronn and Linda found this car in a wrecking yard with a tree growing up through the floor boards. A frame-off restoration began with a Mustang suspension, power steering, and Packard taillights frenched in. The engine is a small block 350 coupled with a 350 transmission and an 8-inch rear end. The keyless entry complements the digital dash. The rear fenders have been widened three inches. Body work and painting was completed by Kevin Van Larrshoven. Upholstery was installed by John Bastoni.

— Ronn & Linda Duty
Billings, Montana

1957 Pontiac Bonneville

Richard & Patricia Proul, Owners

We purchased this 1957 Pontiac Bonneville new from Jim Brooks Pontiac in Helena, Montana. This was the very first year for the fuel-injected Bonneville, all of which were convertibles. The emergence of the Bonneville from an old man's car to a young man's car was made possible with styling that was bolder, more youthful, with performance that would move it to the forefront. Many amenities were added; power steering, electric seats, windows, and an electric antenna. Power brakes and longer leaf springs were added for an easier ride. This car was equipped with a 300 brake horsepower fuel-injected engine, hydraulic lifters and a racing cam. Only 630 of these convertibles left the factory. At $5,782.00, they were the costliest and fastest Pontiac ever made. This fuel-injected version was timed at 18 seconds in the quarter mile. As strictly private entries, these Bonnie cars raced with distinction in NASCAR.

— Richard & Patricia Proul
Helena, Montana

1969 Ford Mustang Mach 1

Irun & Renee Kiljander, Owners

We were honored when our 1969 Ford Mustang Mach 1 won the "2006 Wyoming Muscle Car of The Year" award in Riverton, Wyoming, at the Rebels Rocky Mountain Car Show. It's not every day you see an original car tweaked out to look better than when it was produced. The vehicle data tells it all: Sports Roof, Mach 1, Candy Apple Red with a Black Shaker Hood. This Mach 1 Luxury deluxe interior coupled black vinyl and black vinyl knitted trim. The engine is a 351 Winsor V8 with a 4-barrel and 4-speed close ratio transmission hooked up with a 3.25:1 traction-loc rear end. There were only 72,458 Mach 1s made in 1969. Weight was 3,175 pounds and sold for $3,139 or to look at it another way, just $1.01 per pound!

— Irun & Renee Kiljander
Gillette, Wyoming

Miscellaneous Vehicle Data

Body:	63C	Sports Roof, Mach 1, Deluxe Interior
Color:	T5	Candyapple Red w/Flat Black Hood
Trim:	3A	Black Vinyl and Black Knitted Vinyl, Mach 1 Luxury
Date:	25B	February 25, 1969
D.S.O.:	33	Detroit
Axle:	R	3.25:1, Traction-Loc
Trans:	6	4-Speed Close Ratio

Warranty Number: 9F02M162880

Year	9	1969
Plant	F	Dearborn, MI
Body Series:	02	Sports Roof
Engine:	M	351 4v V8
Unit:	162880	162880

1965 Ford 1/2 Ton

Jerry & Cary Frank, Owners

It Stays In The Family... Memories of a lifetime are wrapped up in our 1965 Ford 1/2 ton pickup. This truck and the I-Beam suspension developed by Ford in about 1960 have proven themselves over the years. This truck, which originated in the Lone Star State of Texas, made it to Montana where it was traded in at Laurel, Montana. My father, Herman P. Frank, purchased this in 1968 for $1,200.00. The truck had a 352 engine with a 3-speed gear shift on the column. It was dad's pride and joy before it became ours. My two older sisters drove the truck to high school before it became my very first vehicle. I almost sold it twice, but my mother talked me out of it. It was about this time we decided to keep it in the family. After restoration, we installed a 390 cubic-inch engine with a C6 automatic transmission. We have lots of memories with this truck and stories we could tell.

— Jerry & Cary Frank
Columbus, Montana

1930 Chevrolet Coach
Joseph & Dixie LaBrie, Owners

For the one who loves classic cars, their eye will always be on the lookout for that special one. This was the case with Joseph and Dixie LaBrie when they found their 1930 Chevrolet Coach at a flea market while shopping in 1997. This car had been kept original in every detail except for upgrading the material on the seats. When they purchased this car, it was about 90% complete, so they had very little work to do to enjoy it. The car had a frame-off restoration, which included the complete power train. They kept the original 216 cubic-inch engine and 4-speed transmission. They loved her from the moment they took her home. She is so much fun to go to the lake for picnics and to remember how their grandparents lived, loved and enjoyed life back in the 1930s. This jewel has been smiling ever since and so have the LaBries.

— Joseph & Dixie LaBrie
Billings, Montana

1930 DeSoto

Wally & Nancy Hammett, Owners

I was born to Mr. Chrysler and Mrs. Plymouth. I came with 18" wheels and a 6-cylinder engine. I have a 6-30 air conditioner – 6 windows down at 30 mph!

I was reborn in the 1990s as a street rod with a 1978-440 with 71 heads, bored .030 over, isky cam and hopped up a little bit. I ride on an all MOPAR suspension, 76 New Yorker 276 gears, 79 Volare front clip, 30 gallon fuel cell and have a new interior, installed in 2006.

I have a touch of road rash, but I'm not too bad for one who was "born" when there were only 48 states and has survived Prohibition, the better part of the depression, a world war, several armed conflicts and seen 14 presidents. These days, I just enjoy the open road...I'm a driver.

I owe a special thanks to the family; Dan, Tana, James, Kyle and Nancy. I also thank Val's Radiator, Caspers Welding, Town & Country Upholstery and the many others who have made certain I'll be around for quite a few more years.

– 1930 Desoto
Wally & Nancy Hammett
Roundup, MT

1929 Ford Model A Sedan
Bob & Gloria Keller, Owners

A work of art, a labor of love, this car can best be described only by the husband and wife who built this yellow sedan with a black vinyl top. If we were to put a price on the hours of labor put into building a car like the professionals do, at $90 to $120.00 an hour, we could not afford to do it.

This classic has a 305 Chevrolet with a 350 turbo automatic transmission. It drives like a dream with the 1966 Corvair front clip with Mustang 11 rack and pinion steering. It has a Ford 8-inch differential, triangulated 4-bar coiled suspension in the rear. To add to the beauty, this street rod has a chopped top.

— Bob & Gloria Keller
Lewistown, Montana

1971 Ford Mustang Convertible

Dennis & Judy Flaig, Owners

When Dennis & Judy purchased this car for just $2,500.00 from Mike Miller in April of 1995 it was in very poor — but restorable — condition. They traveled to Columbus, Ohio to get it, driving it home to Glendive, Montana. During the next few years it was driven very little as it still had a smashed rear quarter panel from the former owner. They placed it in storage for two years before restoring it for their enjoyment. They drove it to Columbus, Ohio where they placed it with KAR Mustangs to under go a complete frame-off restoration. The result was nothing short of perfection from the body work and paint, to the top and new black interior. The Ford 302 c.i. gave all the power they wanted and good fuel mileage. They are now able to enjoy going to car shows like "Cars In The Park,",Glendive, Montana and "Burn the Point" held in Billings, Montana each year.

There were only 6,121 Mustang convertibles made in 1971 costing just $3,227 at the factory plus freight which added to the price as the car weighed in at 3102 pounds. Mustang's grew in size during this model year, becoming eight inches longer and six inches wider and gaining six hundred pounds. Styling was improved, including busier sheet metal and a new front end — bolder with aerodynamics.

— Dennis & Judy Flaig
Glendive, Montana

1954 Chevrolet Bel Air 2-door

Gimmer Robison, Owner

In 1953 Chevrolet got a major face lift, which carried over to the 1954. The Bel Air was the top of the line and came with a higher compression Blue Flame Six that produced 115 brake horse power with a stick shift. Chevy set the pace for production once all the restrictions of World War 11 were over. During 1954, over 1.7 million units were sold, giving General Motors the boost they so badly needed.

When Gimmer was able to get this Classic Car in 1972, he had his work cut out for him. He knew what had to be done if he was going to make this car into a true show car that he could be proud of. He employed a premier body man and master craftsman, Ron Kellum. All the work in the world would be for naught without a showroom paint job to catch one's eye. Gimmer chose Randy Schardein to paint this Chevy in a stunning Mexicali Red . Carol's upholstery did a superb job making this an award winner at car shows. The power plant is the original 235 with 3/4 race cam.

Chevrolet produced 143,573 with a price tag of $1,830.00 plus freight charges.

— Gimmer Robison
Billings, Montana

1953 Cushman Scooter
K. Dan & Jeanette Koch, Owners

Model "Barrel Spring Eagle"

Completely restored from the frame up, this scooter still has its original drive train. A few enhancements have been added: chrome, burgundy red paint and the naugahyde seat cover, which was dyed in a checkerboard patern. This "leg-over" Barrel Spring Eagle model came with an 8-horsepower cast-iron engine and a centrifugal clutch with a 2-speed transmission. The top speed is approximately 40 miles per hour...with a good tail wind! It originally came with a sidecar, which was used primarily as a delivery vehicle. I have the sidecar and it will be refurbished and painted to match.

— K Dan & Jeanette Koch
Laurel, Montana

1963 Mercury Comet
K. Dan & Jeanette Koch, Owners

The Mercury Comet was considered a classy economy car of the 60s. We rebuilt the original 6-cylinder engine (170 CI = 101 horsepower) and the original Dagenham 4-speed transmission, and resealed the original rear axle 3.50:1. Enhancements include: new interior upholstery, carpet, convertible top and boot, chrome grill, chrome bumpers, body chrome, engine chrome, and chrome reverse wheels with Baby Moon Hubcaps and raised white-letter tires. A new AM/FM/CD remote-controlled radio (the original AM radio still worked!) and we added and "OOO-GAH" horn just for fun. We repainted the interior and exterior with the original color – "Carnival Red." I added an exhaust header (Clifford 6=8) with dual muffler and exhaust piping with chrome turn down tips, a new Holley Carburetor (21 mpg), and electronic ignition with 7mm plug wires, which added approximately 30 horsepower.

— K Dan & Jeanette Koch
Laurel, Montana

AUTHOR'S NOTE: Ford Motor Company only produced 5,757 of the S-22 convertible coupe for 1963. The car weighed in at 2,710 pounds and had a price tag of $2,710.00. Ford Motor Company decided to make the Comet its only small car, which turned out to be a very good business decision as the Comet sold well.

1966 Chevrolet Chevelle
Joe & Kim Fuda, Owners

Meet the pride of the fleet – a magnificently restored 1966 Chevelle Pro-street machine.

The garnet red pearl Sikkens paint makes this car a special eye candy treat. A very special thanks for ace mechanic Steve Henle of "The Shop" Stevensville, Montana.

In 1966 this car sold new for just $2484 and weighed in at 3075 pounds. The number of cars produced in 1966 is unknown.

A special note: Kim & I love cars and have always had a great ride. It took a lot of years to build our dream car. This Chevelle makes me feel 16 again and is by far the best ride we have ever had.

— Joe & Kim Fuda
Alberton, Montana

- GM 502 Mark V Blown 1025 raw horsepower
- 847 hp at rear wheels @ 5900 rpm
- torque at rear wheels 759 ft lbs @5600 rpm
- B&M 6-71 mega blower w/3 inch drive belt
- Work done by ABS Competition
- 2-750 Holley carbs for blower w/ 930 flowed cfm
- Cam button. Lumati valve springs.
- Fluidampner
- Moroso flex plate
- Edelbrock victor polished aluminum water pump
- Tilton Super Starter
- Moroso oil pan
- Griffin 4 core aluminum radiator w/two electric fans.
- Barry Grant hot rod 220 gph fuel pump & regulator
- Aluminum fuel log
- This is only about 1⁄4 of items on this fine Pro-street machine

CHEVELLE
Blown '66
Chevy Chevelle

1957 Chevrolet Bel Air
Jay & Tamie Faw, Owners

If we had a crystal ball in 1957, we would have known this car was destined to become one of the world's most admired classics.

After acquiring this car in 2001, Jay & Tami have given it their own personal touch. The interior has the look of the 57's while adding a tilt wheel and Dakota Digital gauges. The Camaro front end supports a very clean 502 cubic inch created engine with 550 lbs. of torque. It produces 450 horse power and a stainless steel exhaust system. It uses a narrowed 9" Ford rear end. Power steering and four wheel disk brakes add to the enjoyment of driving. The paint is a stunning storm gray color. Jay has hidden the battery in the trunk along with a 6 CD changer and a 500 watt amp. Restoration of the body was a full rotisserie with painting by Ron & Vic's Auto Body & Painting.

— Jay & Tamie Faw
Billings, MT

1954 Chevrolet Pickup
Mark & Heide Ventling, Owners

When Mark & Heide purchased this truck back in 2002 at an auction they never dreamed it would become what it is today. They paid $4000 for it and for the next year or so it remained parked in their barn getting driven very little. One day Mark decided it was just not that much fun. There just wasn't much excitement in doing 55 mph tops! The work then began in earnest with a frame-off restoration, adding a 350 blown small block, turbo 350 automatic and a 9 inch Dana rear end. Thanks to Loren Chase of Billings, Montana, this interior is one of the finest and will compete with the very best from coast to coast. Mark & Heide also wish to thank Kevin of Kevin Customs for an unbelievable paint job. A painter for many years, he has became a true professional with the ability to produce top quality show cars and trucks. In 1954, the Chevrolet pickup received its first major restyling with a large triple row of horizontal grille bars bisected with a vertical bar. Chrome grills were rare due to the increased cost, most all were just painted. The parking lights were incorporated in the new grill and were the same ones as used on the GMC of this same year.

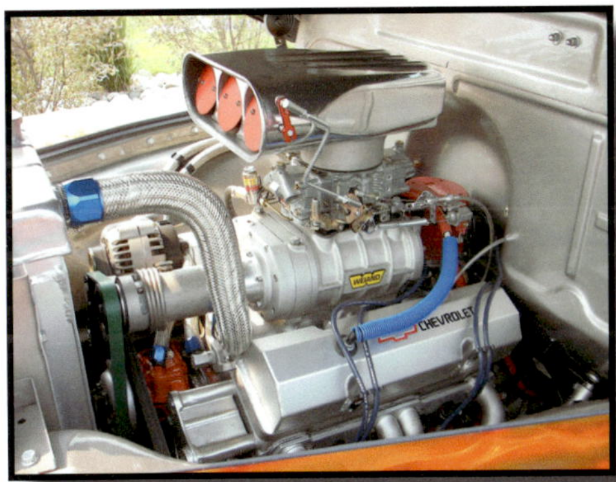

— Mark & Heide Ventling
Laurel, Montana

1953 CHEVROLET CLUB COUPE
FRED & ANN WILSON, OWNERS

This car reflects the smooth clean lines that were the hallmark of General Motors design in 1953 with minor changes in the 1954 models.

The proud owners of this beautiful car they call Creampuff, are Fred & Ann Wilson of Billings, Montana. The original 235 cubic inch 6 cylinder engine still purrs like a kitten. They retained the 3-speed column shift along with the 3:70: 1 differential for good highway performance. When a car like this has endured 53 years only to be in better condition than when it was new, the 103,000 miles becomes only a number to reflect on given the endurance of time. The original tube 6-volt radio, which only has AM, is hard to believe for the generations that have followed who now have FM, CD, DVD players as the norm in today's world.

This was a very popular car with 247,455 built costing just $1707.00. We had little - if any - financing to buy a new car, the result was "no money-no car."

— Fred & Ann Wilson
Billings, Montana

1957 Chevrolet Bel Air
Wayne & Roxanne Hogan, Owners

Cars of the past have a unique place in our hearts, they bring back the treasures of our youth and for a brief moment we are 16 again. This is true with Wayne and Roxanne who own this beautiful 1957 Chevrolet Bel Air Hardtop Sport Sedan. They purchased this car in California in 2000, restoration was a frame on as the car was rust free and in good shape. This 350 cubic-inch engine comes with a mild cam, camel hump heads and 4 bolt mains. With the 750 CFM Holley air gap manifold it cranks out at least 300 horsepower.

In 1957 a total of 137,672 of these cars were produced by General Motors, selling for $2,299.00. Freight generally added about $350.00 to this price.

— Wayne & Roxanne Hogan
Billings, Montana

1934 Ford Coupe
Tom McGarry, Owner

This beautiful green 1934 Ford Roadster is the result of many hours of dedicated detail to what was once a "farm fresh" project car. The price paid was $250 in 1968, which at that time, was considered to be a lot of money. All of the body work, upholstery and paint were completed by the owner, Tom McGarry and his wife Rita. This car had a complete, frame-off restoration, at which time a 302 V/8 was installed using a C-4 transmission and an 8-inch rear end. When Ford produced these cars, they ran over 100 mph with their new flat head engine. They are as popular today as they were then.

— Tom McGarry
Butte, MT

1956 Ford Town Sedan

Susan Buerkle, Owner

A 1956 Ford Town Sedan is a beautiful car built for six passengers to ride in comfort. Susan purchased this Fairlane in 2002 and the interior was completed already. She employed Mike Penni of Modern Auto to do the body work and paint. The car still has the 292 cubic inch Thunderbird engine it came with. Mileage is about 10 mpg; when this car was new, gas sold for about 25 cents per gallon. Many of the cars had 3-speed column shifts and overdrives in the 50s. Lee Iacocca, then a young man, came up with some of the first financing by offering a new 1956 Ford for $56.00 per month. Ford featured a dish steering wheel, but the padded dash and sun visors cost $16 extra, crash-proof door locks were standard. Suppliers were overwhelmed at the demand for seat belts and could only deliver 20% of Ford's requests. Their cost was an extra $9.00. The new curved windshield added style and better vision. Production of the Town Sedan was 254,437 and cost about $1,960 with the weight of 3,201 pounds.

— Susan Buerkle
Park City, Montana

1928 Ford Model A
Judith Wallinder, Owner

Judith Wallinder, a prominent businesswoman in the insurance industry, always wanted a 1928 Ford Model A. This just happened to be the year that the company she represents was founded. She located this truck in Glendive, Montana on a ranch and offered to buy it from the owner for $10,000, even though it was in very rough condition. The sale was delayed for some time as the truck was still being used on a daily basis. When she did acquire it, the job of restoring this vintage truck was left in the hands of Ken Petro, professional mechanic and for many years, the head of the body shop for the Dodge dealership in Billings, Montana. This truck is the centerpiece of her office, which was built around the masterpiece.

In 1928, it was fashionable to be seen riding or - even better - driving a Model A. Franklin D. Roosevelt, who later became President of the United States, purchased one to ride around his Hyde Park Estate in New York City. It had a four-cylinder engine, which was rated at 40 horsepower, and was equipped with mechanical brakes. It was considered top-of-the-line.

— Judith Wallinder
Billings, MT

1955 Chevrolet Bel Air

Ken & Sandy Kunkel, Owners

I was 14 when I got my first car. I still had to wait a full two years before I could drive. The car was a 1955 Chevrolet Bel Air 2-door hardtop with a 327 power plant. For me, time just seemed to stand still as I thought the day would never come when I could get my Montana driver's license. I must admit those two years were well spent fixing this car up and making it my own. I look back now and am amazed at what I started with and what the end result was. The 327 cubic inch engine in this car came out in 1962. The power ranged from 250 to 375 horsepower depending on which carburetor was used. It would produce about 360 pounds of torque at 3600 rpm. This 327 was used in many Corvettes from 1963 to 1968.

At the age of 17 I foolishly sold this car to buy a motorcycle. I regretted that sale for 30 years until I found it for sale and purchased it immediately. This great 55 is fully restored giving us a great ride, which we enjoy to the fullest.

— Ken & Sandy Kunkel
Billings, Montana

1964 Pontiac Tempest GTO
Roy R. Wherley, Owner

Real excitement was in the winds when General Motors introduced the 1964 Pontiac Tempest GTO. This car, purchased in 1973, is completely stock except for the wheels. In 1964, the wheelbase was lengthened to 115 inchs, placing this car in the intermediate series. The corporate A-Body was shared by the Chevelle, Olds F-85/Cutless and Buick/Skylark. The GTO was well accepted when introduced during mid-year production. It was to become the first of the "Muscle cars" and would deliver unprecedented performance in a six-passenger sedan. You were able to "build" your GTO in 1964 starting with a Tempest coupe, hard top or a convertible. You would add the GTO package, floor shift, 389 V8 with tri-power –"optional," and quick steering. The package also included stiff shocks, dual exhaust and premium tires, all at an extra cost of $300. Many other options were available to the new owner like a 4-speed gear box, metallic brake linings, heavy duty radiator and a limited slip rear end. All the driver had to supply was a lead foot and an unlimited supply of gas. The GTO was compared by many to the Ferrari by saying it could beat it in a drag race. This license plate says it all on Roy's classic, -324S389--

— Roy R. Wherley
Three Forks, Montana

1935 Ford with Teardrop Trailer

Jack & Linda Bailey, Owners

This 1935 five window coupe, known as Black Jack, was purchased in 1973 for $800 and it was in very rough condition. It would not run and did not have any interior. Jack and Linda had the foresight that only the classic car lover possesses when it comes to knowing what is junk and what can be salvaged. It all started with a complete frame-off restoration and they added a Mustang II rack and pinion sub frame. By doing this they were able to have disk brakes, power steering and a wonderfully smooth ride. Next came the 350 Chevy small block, a 350 turbo automatic transmission and a 1955 Chevrolet ten-bolt rear end. With the running gear complete, their energy turned to completing the body. Jack had the knowledge and talent to do the body work and prepare it for the paint shop. Sunrise Auto Body & Paint of McClery, Washington went with a brilliant black while adding flames and stripes to give it a true show car appearance. The upholstery was installed by Creek Side Upholstery of Shelton, Washington. Their Black Jack teardrop trailer adds the final touch so many of us strive for.

— Jack & Linda Bailey
Shelton, Washington

1965 Chevrolet Pickup
Wayne & Roxanne Hogan, Owners

This is best described as a true classic pickup. It was a workhorse for the farmer, contractor and those who had to rely on a dependable truck to make their living. This pickup is all original with its paint and upholstery. The tires and wheels are upgrades, however the originals are in a safe storage for a later time. The 292-cubic-inch 6 cyl. engine produces 170 horsepower. My father bought it new for $2,750.00. It has only 36,000 original miles.In 1970 I became the second owner and hope it will always remain in the family.

— Wayne & Roxanne Hogan
Billings, Montana

1937 LaSalle
Dick Harris, Owner

The 1937 LaSalle convertible was the product of designer Harley Earl, who was one of the most respected men of his time in the automotive field. His career stared as a young man in his father's carriage shop. Schooled at Stanford, Earl chose to use clay in the designing of the cars he dreamed of making. His influence for design spans 40 years of American car production. The LaSalle was created as a masterpiece to be a less expensive model of the Cadillac. Many of the appearance features were derived from the Hispano-Suiza. The engine was a 5-litre V8. It became the first car to be mass produced with success. Buick and Oldsmobile were to share the same body sheet metal. Production was halted in 1940, when the LaSalle did not have anything more they could offer to General Motors Cadillac Division. Dick and some of his very close friends completed a frame-off restoration and kept this car its original color.

— Dick Harris
Billings, Montana

1930 Willys Knight Roadster 66-B
Al Giddings, Owner

This beautiful Willys Knight Plaidside Roadster is one of eight known to exist. Owner Al Giddings of Pray, Montana spent 3,600 hours doing the ground up restoration. An 87-horse power Sleeve Valve engine powers all five of the 1930 66-B line of cars. Willys Knight cars of the 1930's were called Silent Knights for the whisper quite performance. 100,000 miles was not uncommon without an overhaul. Giddings, an avid collector of Willys Knight cars, is currently planning to restore all the 1930 66-B line... consisting of a Plaidside Roadster, Plaidside Phaeton, Sedan, Coupe and Great Coupe, a collection that will certainly be a crowd pleaser.

Restoration team: Al Giddings, Jim Selfridge, Dick Thompson, Ernie Schultz. Advisors: Jerry Szostak, Dick Hamilton, Greg Gumtow, Duane Perrin, Joe Lucks.

— Al Giddings
Pray, Montana

1930 Willys Knight 66-B Plaidside Phaeton

Al Giddings, Owner

A rare and stunning Willys Knight touring car, this 1930 66-B Phaeton is the only one known to exist. Three of these beautiful touring cars were built for the 1930 auto shows in New York, Chicago and Los Angeles. A small run of eight right-hand drive Phaetons were built for export, none survived. This car is currently undergoing a full restoration and will be a Pebble Beach candidate in 2007. The famous auto designer, Amos Northrup, designed the 1930 66-B line of cars. This Phaeton is one of the most coveted cars in the Willys Knight registry. Like its Roadster sister, it's a full CCCA Classic.

— Al Giddings
Pray, Montana

1930 Willys Knight Sedan 66-B

Al Giddings, Owner

This Willys Knight 66-B Sedan is one of the 1930 line of cars designed by Amos Northrop. The Willys Knight's are known for their pioneer work using pressed steel. Many car makers in the past used metal that was hand-beaten into shape for their body panels. From 1909 to 1936, the English Daimler Company produced the sleeve value system for their engines under a license agreement with Knight during these years. The Willys Knight cars of the 1930s are some of the most sought after of all the premier classics. Only a handful of these cars remain today.

1967 Cadillac
Ed & Betty Hall, Owners

This pink 1967 Cadillac convertible brings back memories of Elvis Presley when he drove one early in his career. Betty & Ed purchased this gem in fair condition back in 1995. As a master body and paint man, he completed the restoration work himself. The engine is a whopping big 429 cubic inch. The transmission and rear end are stock. The pink peddle car, continental wheel kit and the beautiful white sidewalls add to the allure of this dream catcher. Betty and Ed loved to be called on each year by the local high school to use their Cadillac convertible. It's great for events like homecoming parades as well as other occasions where this beautiful convertible can be used by cheerleaders and prom queens.

In 1967, Cadillac styling received a forward racked grill and front fenders, which were thrust forward. New features included Mylar printed circuits for the instruments, automatic level control, cruise control and a tilt steering that telescoped. This new DeVille convertible cost about $5639 when it came off the assembly line, where production reached just 18,202. Many years ago Cadillac set the standard for luxury cars.

— Ed & Betty Hall
Butte, Montana

1936 Chevrolet Coupe
Herb Stoick, Owner

Classics that are restored come from many places. This 1936 Chevrolet five-window coupe, which was dragged from a riverbank in 1975, was a sorry site being upside down and placed there to eliminate riverbank erosion from the Clarks Fork. Many long hours went into this car to keep it original. The 207 cubic inch six cylinder was able to once again run with the best. The 4-speed floor shift transmission and stock rear end were rebuilt to create a nostalgic driving experience. With the frame-off restoration, mohair upholstery, and Willow Green color, this stock factory car looks new again. Herb's passion in life is automobile restoration.

In 1935, toward the end of the Great Depression, Chevrolet started producing cars again. By the start of production for 1936, Chevrolet produced its ten-millionth car. Most restorers consider this car a difficult restoration because of the wood frame work, which must be rebuilt.

—Herb Stoick
Laurel, Montana

1939 Chevrolet Pickup
Charlie & Eileen Fisch, Owners

Yes, we had to step back for a second look. This 1939 Chevrolet one-ton farm truck has been transformed into a mini semi. The frame was extended by adding two 1983 one-ton rear axles and a one-ton front axle. A sliding fifth wheel, disk brakes and air-ride suspension were installed. A late-model Kenworth sleeper with full custom interior was mounted to the chassis. There is power to spare with the newly created 502 big block, delivering 434 horsepower and 550 foot pounds of torque. The fuel system is comprised of a Quick fuel 4 barrel carburetor, electric fuel pump, old school tunnel ram intake manifold and twin 35 gallon polished fuel tanks.

A custom built 40-foot step-deck flatbed trailer, air ride suspension, Spicer axles and 14-inch tires complete this show piece. This entire unit has been scaled down to 28% the size of a full-size semi. When it was parked between two large semis at a truck stop, it looked like a toy.

— Charlie & Eileen Fisch
Townsend, Montana

1966 Plymouth Belvedere

Karmen & Carolyn Brooks, Owners

The 1966 Plymouth Belvedere two-door hardtop remained a top-of-the-line design for the new model year. This was considered a mid-size car, as it was built on a 117 inch wheelbase — one inch longer than the previous year. When this car was acquired in 2002, it was in very bad shape, to say the least. Work started with Ron Ruski doing the body and paint restoration. Milo's upholstery designed and fabricated the interior. Then came the power, a 440 supercharged engine hooked up with a 727 automatic transmission and 3:93 gears. Karmen & Carolyn finally had their dream car. Plymouth gained a great reputation for street rods with its large choice of big block options available. These muscle cars came with stiffer suspension and oversized brakes to cope with the awesome power that they produced. To this day, the Belvedere remains one of the cars most sought after by collectors. Many of these cars have found a home on the drag strips of our great nation, competing with the very best. Plymouth made 36,644 units selling for about $2,430, plus any options available.

— Karmen & Carolyn Brooks
Boyd, Montana

1956 Chevrolet Bel Air
Rita McGarry, Owner

Rita acquired her 1956 Chevrolet dream car in October of 2000. It looked great, but definitely was not a driver. With the help from her husband Tom, they went through this car with a fine-tooth comb. They rebuilt the Chevy 327 engine along with the 350 turbo automatic. A Ford 9-inch rear end became their choice to make this car into the driver they wanted. Having her own car to work on has been very rewarding. She did all the upholstery herself and it has a professional appearance.

Chevrolet referred to this car as "The Hot One's Even Hotter" with its facelift for 1956. The lines are smooth and flowing. The front end gives that forward look while sporting a lot of chrome. A hidden gas cap is located behind the left taillight. The four inch longer hood has a chrome "V" on the V8 models along with the Chevrolet emblems on the front and rear deck. General Motors' $40 million dollar restyling paid off by making all models look more like the Cadillac. Rita's Bel Air two-door sedan sold new for about $2,025 with production of 104,849 units. Built on a 115-inch wheelbase, it weighed 3,187 pounds.

— Rita McGarry
Butte, Montana

1937 Ford Slantback
Charlie & Eileen Fisch, Owners

So many items went into this 1937 Ford All Steel Slantback, it would take three pages to list them all. This car was restored in only five months. It was chopped 3 inches by Donn Lowe. Bill Hall Body & Frame completed bodywork. Bill Hall & John Doyle did the painting with Mitch Kim doing the striping. Dave Feeken was the master craftsman for the upholstery, featuring sculptured seats and interior. This car has a 1994 Corvette LT-1 350, aluminum 700 R-4 with overdrive and a Jaguar rear end, all highly polished. This car has four-wheel disc brakes, Billet steering wheel and wheels to match, power rack & pinion steering, and chrome front & rear sway bars on a TCI chassis. It has a custom-made polished gas tank and Griffin radiator. Just about every part of this machine is chrome and polished aluminum. Of all the cars I have had the pleasure of looking at in depth, there are very few with this much detail. It is a work of art. The handmade stainless steel dash has classic gauges. Machined aluminum foot pedals and air conditioning provide comfort on those long trips to the many car shows we all love to attend.

— Charlie & Eileen Fisch
Townsend, Montana

1922 Hispano-Suiza
Bill & Sandy Culhane, Owners

The Hispano-Suiza H6 was built from 1919 to 1934. During that period, approximately 2,500 cars were produced. When introduced in 1919, there were a number of technical features including: 6-cylinder aluminum engine with 7 main bearings, full pressure lubrication, overhead cam and a 12-volt electrical system. This car also came with 4-wheel brakes. The 16-inch aluminum drums were made with cast-in steel liners. This car holds a patent for power-assisted brakes. The interior is unique to a four-door phaeton. Top speed of this car is about 95 mph, with 135 bhp. The cubic inch displacement is a large 402.6. With a wheel base of 145.201, it is one of the longest cars ever built. The cost of five new Michelin tires is in the range of $2,400. This car exemplifies the quality and excellence of cars produced in the 1920s. The owners have gone great lengths to make this car able to compete in world class events like the Hilton Head Concours and in Hershey, Pennsylvania and North Myrtle Beach, South Carolina.

— Bill & Sandy Culhane
Billings, Montana

1967 Plymouth GTX
Mike Hicks & Marilyn Moe, Owners

Greetings from Michael Hicks & Marilyn Moe with our 1967 Plymouth GTX 2-door hard top.

This car sat neglected in an open air shed for eleven years. We purchased it from the original owner for $300. It was in rough shape and had flared wheel wells and a spoiler on the trunk for drag racing. Nobody really cared back then! The back seat and door panels were in perfect shape – guess they never went to the drive in! We ordered as many parts as our budget would allow for a year. Two good friends, Steve and Justin Cooper helped us put the car together in a mere five days. What fun! The car is far from perfect as none of us had attempted a complicated task before. It's amazing how a classic brings smiles and great conversation. Our longest drive was from Billings, Montana to Virginia Beach, Virginia. So many people asked if we would make it. My reply was "what did they drive in 1967?" This car has all matching numbers, a 375 horsepower 440 engine, 727 transmission geared by a 323 posi-traction rear end. My fastest time at the drag strip was 14.10 at 98 mph. Yep, Marilyn raced it too. We are hooked on 60's muscle cars. Marilyn and I hope you recognize this car at a show and come over to say "hi."

New, this car sold for about $3,178 or about $1.12 per pound.

— Mike Hicks & Marilyn Moe
Joliet, Montana

1930 Chevrolet Deluxe Panel Delivery Van

Harold Ellingson, Owner

This 1930 Chevrolet was found buried in a ditch bank to prevent the soil from washing away. The location was near the town of Roberts, Montana. When Harold found this old truck, it had only enough of the box left to figure out what the original shape must have looked like. This required a complete frame-off restoration while keeping everything stock. It still has the same engine with a 3-speed transmission. He rebuilt the old body using yellow oak from China. He installed an original 1930 radio and equipped it with a 30-foot cord so he could listen to music at picnics, etc. Locking Chevrolet hubcaps and a spare tire and wheel well are part of this classic. New, this truck sold for about $495.

— Harold Ellingson
Billings, Montana

1968 Dodge Dart
Michael L. Martinez, Owner

This 1968 Dodge Dart has undergone many changes over the past several years under the careful guidance of its proud owner. The power of a 440, equipped with a Holley Dominator 1050, a 727 automatic, and an 8-3⁄4 rear end, makes for a very fast car.

When Michael purchased this car in 1986, it was a rust bucket full of dents and painted the most ugly green one could ever imagine. Many people were responsible for making this car what it is today. The bodywork and paint was done by Jim Garretson and the upholstery completed by Mike Martinez. Robert Carlson was the man behind the building of the engine. The roll cage was built by Dean Isreal. Many special thanks to Quentin and Christian Martinez who were there through all the ups and downs. Drag racing depends on the qualities found in a top notch pit crew. L.J.Martinez, Lenny Patterson, Robert Oleson and Ron Price are the best pit crew a driver could have. With their knowledge of speed, this car performs with the best. In the CCR Runs, it will do the quarter mile in 11.98 seconds at 115 mph.

— Michael L. Martinez
Billings, Montana

1991 Buick Reatta

Patricia North, Owner

This is my Buick Reatta. Although I have had many cars designed by my husband, David, this is my favorite, for many reasons.

The car was a gift from David when he retired as Chief Designer for General Motors. We spent 33 years in Detroit, Michigan, and were looking forward to being back in Montana, where a car like this is fun to drive.

Our friends at Buick knew this car was being built for us and did some special enhancements like a "blue printed" engine and special paint, the color of the Montana sky.

David named the car Reatta after one of his favorite Western movies. I helped him with the process of nominating the brand name. I have a lot of memories like that about this car.

We have had many cars and usually keep them for just a short time – this one is a keeper.

— Patrica North
Billings, Montana

1966 Chevrolet Impala SS

Jim & Mileen Vandeberg, Owners

The 1966 Chevrolet Impala SS is in a class by itself when it comes to luxury and style. This SS has a high-performance small block engine coupled with a 350-turbo automatic transmission. The paint and its many layers of clear coat add depth and beauty to this convertible. Typical features included the SS emblems, vinyl bucket seats, and central gear shift console with an optional tachometer. The SS had stiffer springs and metallic brake liners. The ultra-quick power steering had the best performance in the history of Chevrolet. Of the 1.2 million Chevrolets made, 46% were Impalas. The SS convertible sold for $3,199 and weighed 3,600 pounds. There are no exact production numbers available for this SS Impala. Jim's next project is a complete restoration on his 1953 Mercury Monterey convertible.

— Jim & Mileen Vandeberg
Billings, Montana

1954 Ford Club Coupe
Jim & Mileen Vandeberg, Owners

At one time, Jim & Mileen thought about selling their precious 1954 Ford Club Coupe, then reality set in and they just could not do it. When you spend so many hours doing what you really like to do, it makes parting so much harder. In 1995, Jim acquired this car which needed work, yet was all there. He had Al's Body shop in Great Falls shave the door handles, trunk and hood before painting. Next came the 302 engine, C-4 transmission and 9-inch Ford rear end. Adding the 3-inch drop spindles and disk brakes with power steering gave it the look and ride he wanted. Milo's upholstery added the final touch with an all new interior. In 1954, Ford's flathead V8 gave way to the new Y-block V-8 with its 130 bhp and deep crankcase design. The king pin was then replaced with a ball joint suspension. Just 33,951 of these cars were produced with a cost of about $1,733 at the factory.

— Jim & Mileen Vandeberg
Billings, Montana

1969 Dodge Charger Special Edition
Ken & LaDeen Dykema, Owners

We purchased this Muscle car in 2002. It was in good shape mechanically and had an excellent body. Our 1969 Dodge Charger – Special Edition is a powerhouse. Equipped with a 440 magnum, 375 brake horsepower, a 727 torque flight transmission and 373 gears. Amenities include power windows, brakes, cruise control and air conditioning. 1969 brought a bright new addition to Dodge — the Charger hard top coupe with its fastback roofline and hidden headlights. Basic design of this car was for racing as its aerodynamics were designed for NASCAR. With the 440 magnum came heavy duty suspension, wide tires and oversize brakes. The full-length center console with easy-to-read gauges complements the sporty interior with individual fold-down rear bucket seats. This car was built on a 117-inch wheel base. Production of the V6 and V8 Chargers totaled 69,142 models and sold for a base cost of $3,126.

— Ken & LaDeen Dykema
Manhattan, Montana

1981 Chevrolet Corvette
Terrance & Patricia Martin, Owners

This 1981 Corvette was acquired in the spring of 2005 after it had been in storage for a number of years — rough, neglected and forgotten. Worn out parts were replaced and after a lot of TLC and elbow grease, this third generation Corvette is once again an incredible touring car. It sports all available factory options except a leather interior.

Unique and new to the Corvette in 1981 was a fiberglass mono-leaf rear spring weighing only eight pounds. This was a 33-pound reduction from the steel mono-leaf units. Also used for the first time that year was a Dana aluminum-cased differential. Additionally, the new L-81 version of the 350 CID V8 was a little lighter due to the magnesium valve covers and stainless-steel free flowing exhaust manifolds. Transmission is a turbo 350 coupled with a 2.87:1 rear end. Because of strict government horsepower and emission standards of the time, this last-carbureted Corvette was equipped with a new computer. This command control system controls fuel metering, timing, and torque conversion.

— Terrance & Patricia Martin
Emigrant, Montana

1968 Chevrolet Pickup
Roger & Debbie Boom, Owners

The major transformation of this 1968 Chevrolet pickup started when a Yellowstone Park ranger truck was sold to the GSA through Whiting Motors in Livingston, Montana. It saw some very hard use in this law enforcement agency for 10 years. It was purchased at a public auction by my friend Gordon Williamson, who drove it for another 10 years. I bought it in 1992 for $250 in fair condition after selling my 1969 Firebird convertible. Once again I felt the need for the wind in my hair and I knew I needed a new project. After we removed the top from a good cab, we welded the windshield header panel from a Chevy Blazer to the side posts. We then installed a tuned port fuel injected 350 engine. After placing the computer under the dash, we installed a Doug Nash 5-speed transmission.

1992 Chevy truck bumpers were cut and scribed to fit the front and rear. We built a front tilt hood using the stock hood latch with rollers in the rear with guide plates. A reverse-latch tailgate was made out of conduit and tubing with a steel skin. The gas filler was welded shut on the cab and gas tank, installing the gas tank between the rear frame rails. An aluminum tube framework was built for the removable gas cap cover. Another aluminum framework was built for our bi-fold box cover. We covered it with the same material as the top. The seat is from a late model Chevy truck with a power amp and speakers behind the seat. An old Pontiac gave up the tilt; Vega gave up the steering wheel. Our 16-inch wheels added an extra touch.

All the work was completed at home except engine top work, upholstery & aluminum welding. After 14 years in the making — and lots of smiles later — I have the wind in my grey hair again.

— Roger & Debbie Boom
Bozeman, Montana

1956 Ford Sunliner

Paul & Barbara Etchart, Mitch & Donna Etchart, Owners

This 1956 Ford Sunliner convertible, acquired in 1986, has provided us the best enjoyment we could have asked for. We found it in an area that a local rancher used for his junk. Not thinking it would ever run again, the rancher left it to just rust away. The 292 Thunderbird engine produces 200 bph, the automatic transmission is a three-speed. A frame-off restoration was the first order of business. This was completed after spending many long months...and many dollars. Larry Baumgartner did a masterful job painting our dream car. Ford's facelift in 1956 included a few safety features like a dished steering wheel, break-a-way mirror and crash-proof door locks. If you wanted a padded dash and sun visors, you would pay an extra $16; seat belts cost another $9. Only 20% of the 1956 production had seat belts — performance had a higher priority. Ford made 58,147 Sunliners, which sold for $2,395 and weighed 3,384 pounds.

— Paul & Barbara Etchart
— Mitch & Donna Etchart
Glasgow, Montana

ONE-OFF TIN JALOPY
DAVID H. MASTERS, ARTIST

We turned down quite a few cars for this book because they just weren't up to our standards. Somehow, this jalopy slipped past the review committee. It is truly a work of art and was built by David H. Masters of Joliet, Montana. It has its own permanent parking spot in front of another classic... the "Quick Stop Drive-In" located on Highway 212 in Rockvale, Montana.

1956 Ford Fairlane Sunliner Convertible

Dave & Gloria Harmon, Owners

A stunning beauty in factory pink and black, this 1956 Ford Fairlane Sunliner Convertible will turn your head. In the 50s we called this a "chick magnet." Purchased in 1975 after weathering many long years of Montana winters, it underwent a frame-off restoration with body work and painting completed by Bill Hardy Coachworks. All the upholstery was made to look like it was factory, with installation by Vic Krank, a quality man with his trade. With a 312 engine, automatic and the stock rear end, it drives as if it just came off the show room floor. 1956 saw the dish steering wheel, break-a-way rear view mirror, crash-proof door locks and padded dashes as standard equipment. If you wanted sun visors, they were $16 extra with seat belts costing another $9. Performance was stressed over safety, and as a result only 20% of Ford cars had seat belts. History will look back on the 50s as a time when cars were developed with styling and personality that would last for generations. Girls may not have known a boy's name, but they would know him by the car he drove.

— Dave & Gloria Harmon
Billings, Montana

1957 GMC Pickup

Buz Bailey, Owner

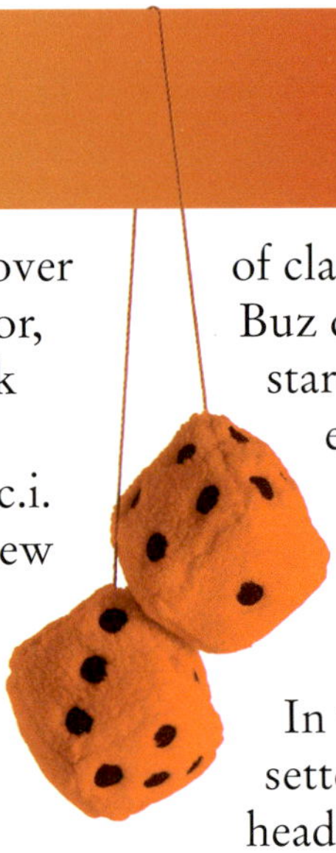

When found, this 1957 GMC was old and rusty. It takes a true lover of classics to undertake a project like this. Beyond the dirt, soiled and worn out interior, Buz discovered that he was only seeing the tip of the iceberg of what must be done. Work started with a frame-off restoration and a lot of ambition. Within one year, a show truck emerged. Trucks like this are expected to have power. He gave it just that using a 350 c.i. small block that makes 368 hp. He added a turbo 350 automatic transmission and a new rear end to make this a true driver. Buz installed the interior to reflect the look he felt a truck like this should have. The body work and paint were completed by Kelly's Kustoms, who once again, demonstrated craftsmanship and professionaism. In the mid 50s,Chuck Jordan, a young designer with General Motors, became a trend setter with his flow through front fender lines, wraparound windshield and hooded headlights.

—Buz Bailey
Billings, Montana

1934 Ford Coupe

Charlie & Eileen Fisch, Owners

The best way to describe this 1934 Ford is just plain "fun." When we purchased this Street Rod in 2003, it was in excellent condition and needed minor work. Body and paint were done by a top-of-the-line restoration shop in Reno, Nevada. A master painter, Brad Cannon, painted this rod and also applied the flames. The engine is a highly polished 350 cubic inch with a 6V671 blower and two 750 Edelbrock carbs. The Dished Blower pistons have a compression of 8.5:1. It has polished Edelbrock heads and a roller cam. We used a Jaguar highly polished rear end with 373 posi-traction gears. The front end has a custom chrome eye beam. Other specialty items include suicide doors, electric windows and air conditioning.

— Charlie & Eileen Fisch
Townsend, Montana

1930 Ford Phaeton
Tom & Tammy DuBoise, Owners

This 1930 Ford Phaeton, known as the "Hulk," is a testament to the man who created it. This car has been transformed in ways very few of us could ever imagine. When you open the driver's door, you see black carpet trimmed in lime green, which is the theme throughout the interior. The dash is custom made of black walnut wood with a natural burl pattern. The Babbet instruments are all customized and set into this beautiful wood. The Hulk is all chrome from the steering wheel to the complete undercarriage. This car has a TCI Racing chassis, a 1969 Jaguar XKE rear suspension and is equipped with a 1932 front dropped axle. The engine is a small block Chevrolet with unique spark plug wires, which allow you to be able to follow the spark from the distributor to the plugs. Travel at highway speeds is made easier with the 700-R-4 overdrive transmission. The most stunning aspect of this car is the $14,000 paint job, which was masterfully done by Cal-Concepts of Bakersfield, California. It incorporated the old- to new-school flames, followed by lightening bolts and blister ghost flames. The "Hulk," painted on the rear, adds a very special artistic touch and thoroughly highlights this beauty's uniqueness.

— Tom & Tammy DuBoise
Great Falls, Montana

1947 Willys-Overland Jeep CJ-2A

Duane & Joanne Demars, Owners

In its day, The Willys Universal earned the title, "Legend." This 1947 CJ-2A spent its life on a farm, where the work was hard and demanding. It was used for farming, hunting and transportation for a young boy to go to school in the 7th and 8th grade. The Jeep was the forerunner of today's modern 4-wheel drive and sold new for about $1,100. The passenger seat cost $8.50; the rear seat cost $10.50. Heaters were extra and produced very little heat. In 1947, a dealership in Lewistown, Montana, sold more Jeeps than any other location in the nation. During World War II, production of all cars, trucks and tractors was suspended. This was due to the need for steel during the war, which was primarily used for weapons. The Jeep took the place of many farming and business needs until American production could catch up to meet our needs as a nation. It had a flat head 4-cylinder engine with about thirty-four horsepower and a three-speed transmission, with a high-low transfer case. Top speed was about forty-five mph. Very few remain of the 113,602 made in 1947 by the Willys-Overland Company.

— Duane & Joanne Demars
Billings, Montana

1951 Lincoln Cosmopolitan Convertible

John & Janet Dougherty, Owners

This Lincoln Cosmopolitan Convertible was considered one of the finest luxury cars produced during the 1950s. In 1951, Motor Trend named Lincoln one of the best cars on the market. John and Janet purchased this automobile in 1974, although it was in very sad shape and needed major restoration. It was parked in a barnyard with the harsh winters taking its toll on every part of it. The chrome, soft top, leather seats and paint all had to be refurbished. John, with his knowledge of automobiles and being a true craftsman, completed all the work by himself. The car has a stock 337 flat head engine (154 horsepower) with the original 3-speed automatic transmission. Out of the 857 Cosmopolitan Convertibles made in 1951, only 17 remain today. The price was about $3,891 and weighed 4,615 pounds. Lincoln had a "sturdy, comfort-secure chassis" complete with skyscraper braced cross members. This type of chassis would filter out any vibration within the car. The Cosmopolitan wheel base was 4 inches longer than the standard Lincolns and cost considerably more to produce. In 1951, Ford motor company statistics said they could only produce 6,300 cars a day at full capacity. Enough for statistics — Ford's production reached up to 9,000 a day that year.

— John & Janet Dougherty
Bozeman, Montana

1958 Ford Fairlane 500 Skyliner

Kenneth & Alta Davidson, Owners

One of the more unique cars ever made by Ford was this 1958 Ford Fairlane 500 Skyliner. It became the first retractable hardtop ever to be mass produced. Today, the Skyliner is one of Ford's premier collectible hardtops. Ford made just 14,713 of these cars in 1958, selling for about $3,163 at the factory. Fender skirts and a continental wheel kit added extra flash and style to this Fairlane's long and low appearance. New styling took a giant step forward and most car makers adopted the quad headlights in 1958. Every year brought major changes. With this car, Detroit proved it had the design team and the engineers with the knowledge to build cars of the future. This car added 4 inches to the length and was 3 inches lower than the 1956 Ford, which was also a popular car. However, the retractable hardtop was only built for three years. Slow sales of the retractable hardtop led to its elimination. A major design change occurred in 1960.

Kenneth purchased this car in 1997. It was rated "a condition # 6." He added air conditioning, disk brakes, a C-6 automatic transmission and a 3.10 rear end. This car was driven in the movie "Walk the Line," but was eliminated when the final cut was made to the film.

—Kenneth & Alta Davidson
Greenville, Mississippi

1939 Plymouth
Dave & Gloria Harmon, Owners

This 1939 Plymouth convertible was the product of the legendary coachbuilder Raymond H. Dietrich, who headed Chrysler styling at the time. The first item to catch your attention is the strong peaked prow-type front end. Many said it was inspired by the Lincoln Zephyr. It also had a vee'd two-piece windshield. Headlights became rectangular and were made flush within the front fenders. The gear shift moved from the floor to the steering column. A major selling point was the ability to raise and lower the new powered convertible top with out getting out of the car. The rumble seat, better known as the "Mother-in-law" seat, was used on the higher end model cars, which had a 114-inch wheel base.

Dave & Gloria pulled this car out of a junk yard in Townsend, Montana, in the mid 1970s. It went through two restorations; the first time back to the original condition. The second time it was modified for modern driving with a 350 c.i. engine and a 350-turbo automatic using an 8-inch Ford rear end. The final touch was body work by Bill Hardy. Ron Honnelly painted the car and Darrin Collins crafted the upholstery.

There were 5,976 convertibles produced during this model year at a price of $895 FOB, freight was about $50 to the dealer.

— Dave & Gloria Harmon
Billings, Montana

1966 Chevrolet El Camino
Karmen & Carolyn Brooks, Owners

General Motors deemed the 1966 El Camino a great success. They placed a lot of value in having power steering at your finger tips for safety. This El Camino is original with a 327 c.i. making 300 bhp. The transmission is a stock three-speed. This 1966 came with better brakes and stronger suspension than the 1965 model. Electronic ignition came as standard equipment. Also included were double-acting shocks and calibrated high-rated springs. The El Camino actually started out to be a muscle car that happened to have a pickup bed. Standard interior included bucket seats; the console was an add-on for an extra price. GM produced 35,119 units that sold for around $3,100 FOB.

— Karmen & Carolyn Brooks
Boyd, Montana

1957 Chevrolet Pickup

Charlie & Eileen Fisch, Owners

A cool ride by any standard, this 1957 Chevrolet half-ton has it all. We installed a 350 cubic-inch crate motor equipping it with an Edelbrock 600 carburetor and a cast iron crankcase. A Durashine manifold with a mild blower cam gives it just enough acceleration. The 350 turbo automatic transmission makes an excellent choice for over the road trips, which are quite frequent in this family. Steve Johnson did an excellent job chopping the top and then applying a showroom paint job with flames and graphics.

In 1957, General Motors did a mild facelift for this new model, including a new grill and oval fender badges. They flattened the hood and gave it two longitudinal bulges that many used to install the windspit ornaments that were found on the Chevy cars. A collector will give it "thumbs up." It has enormous cargo and people capacity. Replacement parts are in good supply.

— Charlie & Eileen Fisch
Townsend, Montana

1967 Camaro SS
Sky Dykema, Owner

The dream of a lifetime came true when Sky got his completely restored, 1967 Camaro Rally Sport SS in 2004. It was factory equipped with a 350 cubic-inch engine, a turbo 400 automatic transmission and 4.11 gears in the rear end. This makes for one sweet ride. This 350 c.i. produces 295 brake horsepower. Although it was exclusive to Camaro for '67, it was soon to become Corvette's most popular engine. The only way you could have this engine was to order the Super Sport package, which was comprised of stiffer springs and shocks, D70-14 Firestone wide oval tires and SS emblems. Also included were the modified hood with extra sound insulation and the "bumblebee" nose stripes. GM added excitement to the Camaro line with their introduction of the 1967s. General Motors chief designer, Bill Mitchell, watched over every aspect of design and production. This car was considered exactly right. It had a long hood, short deck proportions, and its chiseled profile added enhancement to the low-flowing bodylines. When you add in the Rally Sport package, you received a grill with hidden headlights, tinted glass, air conditioning, clock and cruise control. Other performance items included sintered-metallic brake linings, powered front disk brakes, power steering and much more. New, these cars had a base price of about $2,572. Options could add several hundred dollars to the delivered price.

—Sky Dykema
Manhattan, Montana

1964 Ford Fairlane 500

Craig Smith, Owner

This 1964 Ford Fairlane 500 Sport Coupe is completely stock, including matching numbers for paint, upholstery and the complete power train. Out of the 21,431 Sport Coupes produced in 1964, only 4,000 made carried the original "K Code." Out of that number, only 110 are known to have survived. The beautiful guardsman blue is the original factory color on this car. Craig purchased it in excellent condition in January of 2002. The sports coupe came with sportier trim, bucket seats, a console, and gauges. It was equipped with a 289 Hipo engine, 4-speed top-loader transmission and Ford 9-inch 3:89 rear end. Built for speed, including the stiff suspension for performance, the factory production of this Hipo engine adds about 1 bhp per 1 cubic inch of displacement.

This car originated from southern West Virginia where it was used in drag racing. The original owner, a 1960 Super Stock Drag Racer named Dave Strickler, terrorized the drag strips of the southern countryside with this blue beast. The "289 Hipo" Fairlane was able to knock off what was considered the very best dragsters of that era, which included the high-powered Chevrolet 409. New, this car sold for about $2,500 and weighed 2,945 pounds.

— Craig Smith
Billings, Montana

1967 Chevrolet Corvette
John & Ann Peycke, Owner

To find a 1967 Corvette Sting Ray has proven difficult for so many car enthusiasts. John and Ann Peycke overcame that frustration when they located this classic "Vette," which had been in storage for a number of years. It was in very poor condition: seals were dried up, wiring had to be replaced, the original (L-79) 327 cubic inch/350 bhp needed some serious work. Equipped with a four-speed transmission and 3:70 gears, this car has awesome acceleration and will thrill any car buff. Acquired in 2006, this car was restored at Rimrock Auto Body in Billings, Montana, which included a professional change of color and new chrome. Inside, the interior remained as fresh as when it was new. The Corvette has been refined into a true sports car with independent rear suspension and a frame-mounted differential with U-jointed half shafts on a single transverse leaf spring. Front-to-rear weight distribution is 48/52, changed from the old 53/47 found in earlier models. This sports car weighs a mere 3,000 pounds, and sold for $4,353 new, with only 8,504 ever produced.

— John & Ann Peycke
Billings, Montana

1949 Mercury Coupe
Dick & Diana Anderson, Owners

One of the most beautiful and sought after cars is the 1949 Mercury Coupe. This one is amazing in every way. It is a complete customized version with a chopped top, suicide doors and flame fender skirts. When Jerry purchased this in 2001, he could only visualize what it would look like in the years to come. The ghost flames are some of the best quality I have seen, and from every angle they will look to appear a different shade of blue. From the reset custom tail lights, shaved door handles to the graphics of this car on the fire wall, you will find an eye for detail. The interior can only be described as striking with its blue and white trim through out. When you find a car in great shape like this one was, building it into your dream car is made easier. Retained was the 302 cid and the automatic transmission. Building a car like this may take years and it also takes a loving wife to give encouragement when things are not going well.

— Dick & Diana Anderson
Great Falls, Montana

1957 Plymouth Fury Sport Coupe
Howard & Rosetta Barrick, Owners

The 1957 Plymouth Fury Sport Coupe was a product of chief designer Virgil Exner of the Chrysler Corporation. It was known for its "Forward Look." Purchased in 2000 by Howard & Rosetta, this original Fury is painted off-white with gold trim, a new production color for 1957. Even the air cleaner housing had gold color on this new V-800 dual-carb 318 cid. This engine, new to the Fury hard top, was the biggest in the low priced field. It developed 290 bhp and 320 foot pounds of torque. The transmission was a torque flite push button 3 speed. Designed more than four inches wider and three inches lower with tall "shark" fins it was truly one of the best styled cars of the year. Production was 7,438. Selling at $2,925, built on a 118 inch wheel base it weighed 3,595 pounds.

— Howard & Rosetta Barrick
Bozeman, Montana

1979 Chevrolet Corvette

Craig & Karen Swenson, Owner

This is an original 1979 factory Corvette Coupe. When Craig and Karen acquired it in September of 2004, the actual miles on it numbered only 1,596. This was like a dream come true. They located it in Crosby, North Dakota, where it was in heated dry storage for the past twenty-five years. It was purchased new in Bowman, ND, from Nordberg Chevrolet and trailered to Crosby. This car received excellent care and was serviced annually. The only time it saw daylight was for hometown parades, and yes, many a homecoming queen has ridden in this classic 'Vette over the years.

Every car has a list of the options available to the new owner. When this 'Vette was purchased, it had every option offered. It has the L-82 / V8 350 (5.7 L) 370 bhp. No other engine has captured the heart of the car enthusiast like this small block Chevy. It was no longer offered in models after 2000, however, its production numbers were very impressive with 90,000,000 made over just a few short years. GM small blocks have become the company's corporate standard to this day. With a snow white exterior and brilliant soft red leather seats, this car is among the very few in its original show room condition.

— Craig & Karen Swenson
Billings, Montana

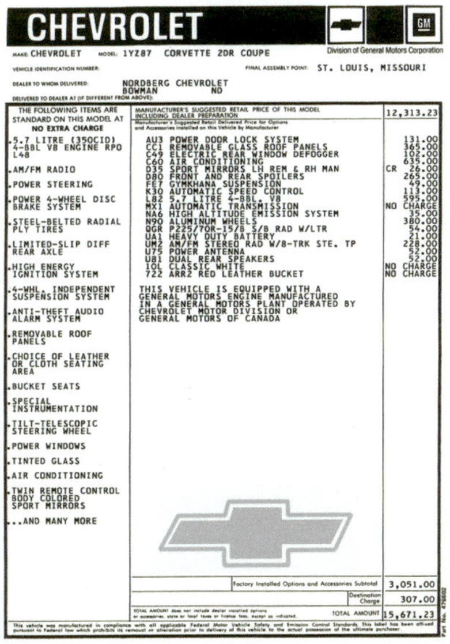

CHEVROLET

Division of General Motors Corporation

MAKE: CHEVROLET MODEL: 1YZ87 CORVETTE 2DR COUPE

VEHICLE IDENTIFICATION NUMBER:

FINAL ASSEMBLY POINT: ST. LOUIS, MISSOURI

DEALER TO WHOM DELIVERED: NORDBERG CHEVROLET BOWMAN ND

DELIVERED TO DEALER AT (IF DIFFERENT FROM ABOVE):

THE FOLLOWING ITEMS ARE STANDARD ON THIS MODEL AT NO EXTRA CHARGE

- 5.7 LITRE (350CID) 4-BBL V8 ENGINE RPO L48
- AM/FM RADIO
- POWER STEERING
- POWER 4-WHEEL DISC BRAKE SYSTEM
- STEEL-BELTED RADIAL PLY TIRES
- LIMITED-SLIP DIFF REAR AXLE
- HIGH ENERGY IGNITION SYSTEM
- 4-WHL. INDEPENDENT SUSPENSION SYSTEM
- ANTI-THEFT AUDIO ALARM SYSTEM
- REMOVABLE ROOF PANELS
- CHOICE OF LEATHER OR CLOTH SEATING AREA
- BUCKET SEATS
- SPECIAL INSTRUMENTATION
- TILT-TELESCOPIC STEERING WHEEL
- POWER WINDOWS
- TINTED GLASS
- AIR CONDITIONING
- TWIN REMOTE CONTROL BODY COLORED SPORT MIRRORS
- ...AND MANY MORE

MANUFACTURER'S SUGGESTED RETAIL PRICE OF THIS MODEL INCLUDING DEALER PREPARATION		12,313.23
Manufacturer's Suggested Retail Delivered Price for Options and Accessories installed on this Vehicle by Manufacturer		
AU3	POWER DOOR LOCK SYSTEM	131.00
CC1	REMOVABLE GLASS ROOF PANELS	365.00
C49	ELECTRIC REAR WINDOW DEFOGGER	102.00
C60	AIR CONDITIONING	635.00
D35	SPORT MIRRORS LH REM & RH MAN	CR 26.00
D80	FRONT AND REAR SPOILERS	265.00
FE7	GYMKHANA SUSPENSION	49.00
K30	AUTOMATIC SPEED CONTROL	113.00
L82	5.7 LITRE 4-BBL. V8	595.00
MX1	AUTOMATIC TRANSMISSION	NO CHARGE
NA6	HIGH ALTITUDE EMISSION SYSTEM	35.00
N90	ALUMINUM WHEELS	380.00
QGR	P225/70R-15/B S/B RAD W/LTR	54.00
UA1	HEAVY DUTY BATTERY	21.00
UM2	AM/FM STEREO RAD W/8-TRK STE. TP	228.00
U75	POWER ANTENNA	52.00
U81	DUAL REAR SPEAKERS	52.00
10L	CLASSIC WHITE	NO CHARGE
722	ARR2 RED LEATHER BUCKET	NO CHARGE
Factory Installed Options and Accessories Subtotal		3,051.00
Destination Charge		307.00
TOTAL AMOUNT		15,671.23

THIS VEHICLE IS EQUIPPED WITH A GENERAL MOTORS ENGINE MANUFACTURED IN A GENERAL MOTORS PLANT OPERATED BY CHEVROLET MOTOR DIVISION OR GENERAL MOTORS OF CANADA

TOTAL AMOUNT does not include dealer installed options or accessories, state or local taxes or license fees, except as indicated.

This vehicle was manufactured in compliance with all applicable Federal Motor Vehicle Safety and Emission Control Standards. This label has been affixed pursuant to Federal law which prohibits its removal or alteration prior to delivery of this vehicle to the actual possession of the ultimate purchaser.

Part No. 476602

1967 Chevrolet Chevelle
John & Ann Peycke, Owners

This 1967 Chevrolet Chevelle 300 was headed for the bone yard back in 1988 when Johnny and Ann saw a diamond in the rough and purchased it. When you have grown up with muscle cars you develop a bond going back to your teen-age years. Rimrock Collision Center was given the task of restoring the body and later giving it a paint job worthy of a true classic. A 396/350 bhp was installed with a turbo 350 automatic transmission. The power train was completed with a posi. 3.73 rear end. Power disc brakes were added along with a stainless steel exhaust system using Flow Master's. General Motors produced about 4,800 Chevelle 300'S with the v8 in both the two and four door models. Built on a 115 inch wheelbase they sold for $2,326 and weighed 3,070 pounds. This car now is true show quality in every respect, proudly owned and loved as a member of the family.

— John & Ann Peycke
Billings, Montana

1957 Chevrolet Bel Air

Ken & LaDeen Dykema, Owners

We acquired this 1957 Chevrolet Bel Air 2-door hardtop in 1982. It is in show room condition and completely stock. The 283 small block with the 4-speed transmission and 411 gears make for smooth driving at highway speeds. There were not many of these cars that had electric windows and electric seats. Like most cars of the fifties era, the '57 Chevrolet would be considered the defining car based on public perception. Only 166,426 of these Bel Air sport coupes were made, selling for about $2,299. The car weighed 3,278 pounds on a 115-inch wheelbase. Typically, they were loaded with many extras, adding large profits for General Motors. Seven engine choices were available from the basic 140 horsepower six, all the way up to the 283-CID V8 "Ram Jet" fuel injection, producing a full 283 brake horsepower. In June of 1957, Chevy became a formidable competitor on the NASCAR track and other stock car events. During the 1957 Daytona Speed Week, cars in Class 5, (259-305 CID) were able to take 33 of the top 37 places. The fastest car averaged a speed of 137.076 mph. In the Pure Oil Manufacturers Trophy point's award, Chevy won 574 points to the runner-up Ford, with 309 points. When these cars were built, the average worker made $4,230 a year. The average family income was $5,034 with doctors earning over $22,000. If you were the everyday workingman, your earnings were about $2.08 per hour. Work for women beyond the family was limited, their wages were much lower than men and the good paying jobs eluded them.

— Ken & LaDeen Dykema
Manhattan, Montana

1960 Lincoln Continental Mark V
Ira & Ona Cuelho, Owners

Classic cars are purchased for many reasons: investments, sentiments, and car shows. This 1960 Lincoln Continental Mark V was special. Ira and Ona bought this car in 2005 as a wedding present to themselves rather than go on a honeymoon. This was the final year for Lincoln's "cat's-eye" styling and a difficult time for Ford Motor Company as sales declined. Size was getting larger. Lincoln was one inch longer than the Imperial and almost two inches longer than Cadillac. Total length exceeded nineteen feet. A 430 cid V8 engine was the largest on the market and mileage was only ten mpg. Interiors were soft top grain leather combined with quality fabrics. Only 2,044 convertibles were produced selling for $7,056. They weighed over two ton.

—Ira & Ona Cuelho
Columbus, Montana

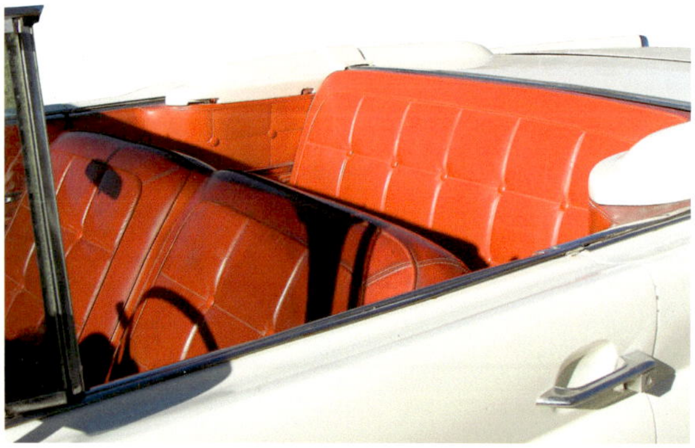

1951 Chevrolet Sedan Delivery

Mick & Lynnette Gainan, Owners

Our dad looked for several years trying to locate a 1951 Chevrolet Sedan Delivery. He wanted to fix it up to look like the original one that he and mom started the business with.

I spotted it in the rear view mirror of a pickup that I was driving. It was in October, 1978. Unfortunately, dad passed away in June 1978, four months before I found this vehicle. Two doors were welded shut, bumpers welded on, roof and hood caved in, motor not running and the oil was like tar. The original 216 engine and three-speed column shift were still in the vehicle. I shared the story of my dad's dream with a group of friends called the Big Sky Street Rod Association, of which I was a member. These guys adopted this project and turned it around in just 45 days, complete with painting, graphics and lettering.

They called this vehicle their "Panic Wagon" and mom was the driver. She handled all the deliveries of flowers daily throughout the community, along with 3 kids bouncing around in the back. The rose etched in the back window was the original logo for our store.

The Gainan's delivery van was presented the 1st Christmas without our dad, in loving memory of "The Founder" to our mom, Betty "Gramma G" (Panic Wagon Driver) Gainan.

— Mick & Lynnette Gainan
Billings, Montana

1955 Ford Fairlane Sunliner Convertible
Dick & Diana Anderson, Owners

This '55 Ford Fairlane Sunliner convertible was purchased in 2005 in great shape. The former owner had spent hundreds of hours to make this car the show piece it is today. It has a custom convertible top with the rear window of the 1940 vintage era. This car has the original 272 cid with tri power set up to produce about 185 plus bhp. The black paint is in very good condition due to only 40,077 actual miles on this beauty. With a new cost of $2,224 this Sunliner out sold the Crown Victoria to the amazement of top management. The continental wheel kit, fender skirts and dual exhaust gives the impression this car is long on style with power to spare. In 1955 only 8% of all households had more than one car. Ford set out to change this with an add campaign of "Fords By The Pair". They suggested a station wagon and a convertible as a perfect match. Ford produced just 49,966 cars weighing 3,315 pounds during this model year.

— Dick & Diana Anderson
Great Falls, Montana

1969 Chevrolet Chevelle 300 Deluxe

John & Ann Peycke, Owners

The 1969 Chevrolet Chevelle was the car that appealed to the young-at-heart when it was produced. Even today it stills appeals to the young-at-heart. This 300 Deluxe version has bench seats and a rare L78/396 CID, producing an astonishing 375 bhp. When Johnny tweaked out this mill using a chambered exhaust, it dyno tested at 425 bhp. Performance was enhanced with the M-21 4 speed transmission and 3.73 posi. rear end. The car was considered in good condition when purchased in 2003. A frame-off restoration was done with body and painting completed at Rimrock Collision Center of Billings, Montana. The interior for the car was installed by Custom Upholstery of Portland, Oregon. This 300 Deluxe was built on a 112-inch wheelbase. 11,000 were made featuring all three models. Base price was $2,521 plus extra for the 396 CID. Dry weight was 3,075 pounds at the factory.

— John & Ann Peycke
Billings, Montana

1932 Ford Victoria

Jerry & Suzy Gray, Owners

"Perfection!"

That would be a great way to describe this 1932 Ford Victoria. Completed in the summer of 2004, it was painted by Jerry Gray and Bret McGinler. The body work was completed by Down's Mfg. using a fiber glass body with extensive support on a TCI "rolling chassis". Interior was installed by C & B Upholstery in Spokane, Washington. During the building of this Street Rod, a 350 Chevrolet Ram Jet engine was installed using a 700-R-4 transmission. A Currie 9" posi. rear end with 3.70:1 gears, 11" front disc and 10" drum rear brakes were added. This car was built with all the amenities to produce an award winning show car. The paint is Vermillion Red/Harley and Vivid black with custom pin stripping by Von Rago of Coeur d'Alene, Idaho. It was chosen to be shown at "Hot Rod's and Harley's" an invitation-only at the Tacoma Dome. In 2005 it won 15 awards in 15 shows/events including "Gotta Drive Em" category at GOODGUYS West Coast Nationals in Pleasanton, CA.

— Jerry & Suzy Gray
Belgrade, Montana

1965 Ford Mustang

Jack & Linda Riley, Owners

The 1965 Ford Mustang proved to be one of the greatest success stories of all time for the automobile industry. Production reached 680.989 from April 1964 to August of 1965 when the model year changed to 1966. This 1965 Mustang is a shining example of how these cars have faired in the world of classics. Purchased in 1988, this car underwent a mild restoration with flared fenders and yellow paint. It sports some awesome flames with graphics of Tweedy Bird. This 351 Winsor has roller rockers, 202 Edelbrock aluminum heads, forged pistons, Mallory ignition, and a Speed DeaMon carburetor. A Currie 9-inch rear end, C-4 transmission coupled with a ratchet shifter are all essential to a super fast Mustang. Auto meter gauges were professionally installed in the stock dash. A Mustang NOS kit placed in the trunk has never been used. A custom interior made for this car adds that special look that show cars strive for. When Mustangs appeared in show rooms across the nation, many accidents happened due to people trying to get a glimpse of them. The demand exceeded Fords production by 15 to 1. Hard top production reached 501,965 and sold for $2,362.

— Jack & Linda Riley
Great Falls, Montana

1940 Ford Sedan Delivery

Mick & Lynnette Gainan, Owners

Very rare, this 1940 Ford Sedan Delivery was purchased in about 1975 after having some major vandalism. Even the primer could not cover the damage done by a hammer to the sheet metal and glass. Many craftsmen were called on to restore this delivery van to its pristine condition. Frame and suspension work was by Don Miller and Jim Larson of Contemporary Metal Smiths; Gordon Peterson did the wiring; Jim Lords did the body and paint; and the upholstery was designed by Steve Radovich of Great Falls, Montana. The power train has a Chevrolet 350 cid/396 bhp, a turbo 400 automatic with a '68 Vette rear end.

In one guy's opinion, *"The beautiful lines of the '40 Fords coupled with the reliability of all Chevrolet power train. It doesn't get any better than that."*(Author unknown) Many designers said it was the best body ever built. It had smooth lines and an art-deco dashboard with contrasting colors. The Sedan Delivery used the same front end as the Deluxe Ford Sedan as its styling was considered the best of the post war era.

— Mick & Lynnette Gainan
Billings, Montana

1929 Ford Model A 170-A Sedan

Craig & Karen Swenson, Owners

This model is one of the rarest of models, primarily because it was first produced in late 1929 and only produced for a few months when the new 1930 models appeared. The model 170-A is referred to as a Blind Back because of the lack of a rear quarter window.

Ford made another four-door sedan without these windows that are sometime confused with the model 170-A. These are the "Leatherback" model 60-A with a brown simulated leather top produced in 1928 and model 60-C, called the Steelback, which also appeared later in 1929 and had no leather on the top, just steel (with the traditional top material in the center, of course).

This Model A was restored by Frank Politelli of Southern California and first shown at the 1998 Reno National Model a Convention sponsored by the Model A Club of America. The cars are judged according to how closely they resemble the condition of the car in comparison to the month and year the car was built and would have appeared in the Ford showroom. This vehicle qualified for blue ribbon judging but was entered in touring class judging at Mr. Politelli's insistence. However the cars are judged the same in both classes. This car received 451 points, well over the 400 out of 500 needed to receive the First Place Award. As I recall, it was the fifth highest scoring car in this national meet, a very impressive achievement! The car was later shown at the Southern California Regional Model A meet held in Temecula, California and also received a first place award. Jim Beley purchased the car shortly after this meet. Craig & Karen purchased this car May 22, 2006.

— Craig & Karen Swenson
Billings, Montana

1922 Chandler Phaeton
Dick Harris, Owner

This 1922 seven-passenger Chandler Phaeton was made only a short time, from 1913 to 1929. It's sad to say that with the crash of the stock market in 1929, also came the demise of a large number of automobile makers. This four-door Phaeton, a very deep wine color, was built to satisfy the most discriminating taste of the well-to-do. The car was well accepted in the market place. during the 1922 production run, Chander offered ten different cars ranging in price from $1,495 to $2,375. Wood framing was still the standard used in production; steel framework did not become the standard until the 1930s. The Chandler engine, called "The Marvelous Motor," was built in Cleveland, Ohio, with 29 horsepower within 4736-cc bi-block six-cylinder. Its serial number is 121210.

— Dick Harris
Billings, Montana

1947 1/2 Ford Coupe

Mike & Laurie Antonio, Owners

It was originally built in Great Falls, Mt. as a Drag Car and purchased from Jim Vandeburg, Billings, Mt.in 2004. It had been sitting in storage for about 5 or 6 years. It came with no engine, a two speed drag transmission and a Dana 60-C 4:10 posi-traction rear end. It hooked me because I really like the 40s coupes that Ford made and I was also Born in 1947. I figured I should have a hot rod born the same year as myself.

It now has an Eldelbrock '79 4 bolt main 350 Chevy crate engine. A mildly beefed up 350 transmission, The same Dana 60-C 4:10 Posi. rear end completely gone through. I added a Gear Vendors Under/Over Drive. That allows it to cruise at freeway speeds and maintain decent gas milage. And yes it will come out of the hole! All new wiring, Dakota Digital Dash, electric windshield wipers, Vintage Air Gen II A/C, Heat and defrost, Walker Radiator, front disk brakes. The suspension is a '79 Monte Carlo front end clip, and G.M.leaf springs rear.

Under Pinnings: Silent Knight Custom Exhaust, Terry Collett, Billings, Mt., • Other Pinnngs: Westside Kustoms, Ron Tesinsky, Billings, Mt., • Transmission: Big Sky Transmission, Ron Struss, Billings, Mt., • Body & Paint: Todd's Paint Shop, Todd, Billings, Mt. • Interior: Jerry's Trim Shop, Jerry Weitz, Billings, Mt.

— Mike & Laurie Antonio
Billings, Montana

1946 Cadillac Gothic Hearse
Jered & Bonnie Scherer, Owners

This 1946 Gothic-style Cadillac hearse is very rare. This is one of three known to exist in the nation.The restoration on this will take at least five years. Many of the original parts are no longer available and must be recrafted by hand. This hearse was purchased in 1992 and placed in dry storage for ten years. It is the first commercial coach chassis built following World War II by its maker, Meteor Coach Company.

— Jered & Bonnie Scherer
Billings, Montanan

1956 Cadillac Superior Hearse
Jared & Bonnie Scherer, Owners

A step back in time lets us take a look at this beautifully preserved 1956 Cadillac hearse by Superior Coach Company. Purchased in 1989, this special edition marked the 50th year of production for Superior Coach Company. As a golden anniversary model, it has a special gold plaque commemorating this milestone. This limousine style was very limited in its production.

— Jered & Bonnie Scherer
Billings, Montana

Index